MW01225798

Dedicated to Lucy Lea Saltzman, who always made sure I had a clean pair of jeans, and Lou Mischkind (1935-2007), a friend who forgot more than I'll ever know.

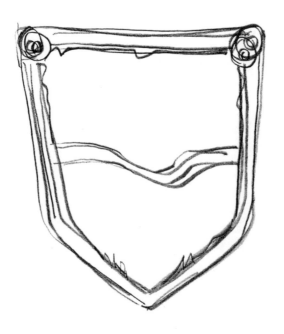

My Jeans Are Irregulars

Volume III

The Third Installment Of Collected Works On Organizational Performance

By Jeffrey M. Saltzman

Frank –
all the Best
Jeffrey Saltzman

Kenexa

Published by Kenexa®
Corporate Headquarters:
650 East Swedesford Road, Second Floor
Wayne, PA 19087
© 2009 Kenexa
All rights reserved.
ISBN 978-0-9800252-3-1
Edited by: Stephanie Sparks and Jennifer Meyer
Creative Direction: Andrea Watkins
Managing Designers: Kendra Erickson and Kara Ruder
Illustrations: Deb Lee
No part of this publication may be reproduced in any form
or by any means without written permission of the publisher. The
content contained, herein, is the opinions of one person and does not
necessarily represent the view of Kenexa or its employees.
www.kenexa.com

Table of Contents

INTRODUCTION

~

FROM THE AUTHOR

One often overlooked aspect of communications or miscommunications is the differing levels of saliency that messages have for listeners. A word, a phrase, a passage, even when defined similarly by differing listeners, may carry with it differing levels of saliency or importance. A line casually thrown out about future opportunities by a person in power for instance, a line that the speaker will have trouble recalling the next day, may become central to a listener's being, the listener hanging his/her hopes onto those uttered words. I would surmise that a portion of the miscommunications that happen in the workplace is not simply due to differing definitions of the messages being conveyed, or unclear messages, but rather something more elemental. Namely, that the same message, with differing emotional content or saliency to various listeners will cause people to put differing emphasis on the importance of the message and create variance on how people act upon the messages received.

Communications are merely a tool. As a hammer is to building a house, how those communications are used in managing is what can lead to higher or lower levels of organizational performance. The essays in this book focus on organizational performance and explore my take on how to enhance that performance gathered from 25 years of examining organizational cultures.

"My Jeans Are Irregulars" is the third in the series which includes, *"A Moose in the Distance And Other Thoughts on Organizational Performance"* (2007) and *"Well, I Guess That Is Not Going to Grow Back"* (2008).

10,000 Children

WEDNESDAY, MAY 28, 2008

PERFORMANCE

In a series of articles, *The Wall Street Journal* wrote a detailed account of how Bear Stearns imploded and left JP Morgan and the Federal Reserve to patch together a solution. The series discussed how Bear's CEO, Alan Schwartz, in meetings with his direct reports, called the precipitous decline in the value of the firm's stock over a short period of time "a whole lot of noise," a reference to a passing moment. Client after client was pulling their assets from the firm, resulting in a modern day version of a run on the bank.

The Wall Street Journal goes on to say that in a business such as Bear's, which relies on trust and relationships, a decline in trust could lead to the demise of the firm. But I don't think that trust or a decline in trust really captures what happened to Bear Stearns. I think a more appropriate concept would be a decline in *confidence*, of which trust is a component. When Schwartz was talking to his direct reports, he was trying to calm their nerves and instill confidence. They likely already trusted him because they had relationships with him and worked with him daily, but what they seemed to lack (according to the article) was confidence that a course was being charted for the firm that would lead it out of its current difficulties and to a successful outcome. The lack of confidence in Bear, by its customers, resulted in a seminal and final moment for that storied institution and its 13,000+ employees.

Confidence, as a broad concept, is defined as a state of being certain that a hypothesis or prediction is correct, or that a chosen course of action is the best or most effective given the circumstances. Confidence can be described as a subjective, emotional state of mind, but can also be described statistically and represented as a confidence level within which you may be certain that a hypothesis will either be rejected or deemed plausible.

Among the deaths counted in the earthquake that ravaged central China's Sichuan province are an estimated 10,000 schoolchildren. This tragedy unfolded slowly and of course was heartbreaking to watch. The parents of the schoolchildren are now taking on an unusual role for people within the communist state, that of protester. Many of them appear to be angry that the schools that served their children, from poorer backgrounds, collapsed in the earthquake to a much greater degree than schools that served wealthier families and other nearby government office buildings. There is speculation that corruption and official indifference caused the schools that collapsed to be built in a substandard fashion. The unstated assumption is that officials either did not care as much about poorer families or thought they could get away without imposing the same due diligence on the buildings constructed to service the poor.

Parents who have lost the one child they were allowed, have lost their sense of future and their confidence that the government was, at least minimally, looking after their interests. (If a child dies and couples are able, they are allowed to have another.) Parents are often willing to put up with much hardship and suffering if they feel they are working toward a better future for their children. The parent protests are increasing, and a riveting picture appearing in *The New York Times* and flashing around the Internet shows a local official on his knees pleading with the parents to discontinue their march and allow the local party to investigate why so many school buildings collapsed. Parents ignored his pleas and continued their march. One public official associated with the schools was quoted as saying that each family would be compensated $4,500, several years' worth of wages for each child that died and as the protests continued over the weeks that number was significantly raised. I don't think the parents are looking for money.

The parents' lack of confidence that the system is looking after their interests and their children in a fair and just manner may be creating a seminal moment for China. But, 10,000 children is a very high price to pay for societal change. When society decides that the price it has paid for the continuation of the status quo is too high, it will change.

On Saturday, March 25, 1911, a fire broke out on the top three floors of the 10 story Asch building located at 23-29 Washington Place, on the lower east side of Manhattan. The incident became known as the Triangle Shirtwaist Factory fire and resulted in the deaths of 148 of the 500 factory workers, who either burned or jumped to their deaths. This was and continued to be the worst industrial accident in NYC until 9/11 occurred. One exit stairway had been chained shut, the flimsy fire escape soon collapsed as people struggled to flee, the elevator stopped working and the remaining staircase was inadequate for the number of people in the building.

The workers were mostly young immigrants, some only 15 years old who toiled for 14-hour shifts, 60-72 hours per week. The average weekly wage was between $6 and $7. After the fire, the owners were put on trial and were acquitted, but then lost a civil suit that compensated the average family $75 for each killed worker, or about 11 weeks' worth of wages. I don't think those parents, survivors or relatives were looking for money. They had lost confidence in the current system, organized themselves and the outrage that followed the deaths caused new and enhanced safety requirements for buildings to be enacted—resulting in the slow improvement of working conditions for factory workers throughout the United States.

> The people demanded restitution, justice and action that would safeguard the vulnerable and the oppressed. Outraged cries calling for action to improve the unsafe conditions in workshops could be heard from every quarter, from the mainstream conservative to the progressive and union press, (Cornell University Archives).

It was another seminal moment, but 148 lives was a very high price to pay for societal change.

Confidence is critical to our everyday lives. Without confidence, not only would many of our institutions collapse, but our society overall would cease to function. Whether you deposit money into a bank is determined by your confidence that the money will be there when you need it, that the bank will not disappear, squander or lose your money. Whether you go to a hospital when you are sick is driven by the confidence you have that going to the hospital would in fact help heal you. Interest in the United States' national elections, the percentage of voter turnout, is clearly dependent on whether voters are confident that their vote is meaningful. Whether you stay with your current employer or seek employment elsewhere is driven by your confidence that you will benefit by staying put or benefit more by going elsewhere. Whether you go to college or not is driven by your confidence that going to college will result in positive outcomes for you personally. The value of our money, our paper currency, is dependent on the confidence people have that the government has the means to stand behind the currency and, to a large extent, confidence in the government itself. When you buy or use a product from a company, you need to have confidence that the product will work as advertised or you would not buy it in the first place. The list could go on and on.

Confidence could be thought of as having two very broad components, organizational confidence and personal confidence. Organizational confidence is confidence in the various organizations or institutions that we interact with, and personal confidence is the confidence in your own abilities. Each of these dimensions has an internal and an external component.

Think of the concept of Employee Confidence. The intersection of Internal and Organizational Confidence covers the quality of the management team and the business processes that are in place. External Organizational Confidence covers the positioning of the organization in its markets and the robustness of the industry in which the organization operates.

Internal Personal confidence covers job security and how bright your future appears at your current employer. External Personal Confidence covers your ability to find another job, comparable to the one you have.

Consumer confidence could be thought of within this framework as well, as could military confidence, economic confidence, political confidence, educational confidence, health confidence and many others. Confidence becomes an over-riding rubric allowing various slices to be defined and measured. Each type of confidence may predict varying societal outcomes or organizational performance depending on how it is defined and measured.

Generational Differences at Work

Saturday, May 3, 2008

Organizations

"They poison the mind and corrupt the morals of the young, who waste their time sitting on sofas immersed in dangerous fantasy worlds."

What is this statement decrying? At first glance, you might assume video games, but it was written in the 1700s. It was aimed at a new medium that was springing up at the time, a medium that the older generation was lamenting was going to be the ruin of the younger generation—novels. Today of course, we would be thrilled if the younger generation became immersed in novels and were hooked on reading; it would be considered a virtue.

Whether it is novels, motion pictures, cars with rumble seats, rock and roll, hip-hop, tattoos, green and orange hair or body piercing, the older generation has looked at the younger generation and has always seen peril in the different fads or standards that are adopted. One has to wonder if it has more to do with the younger generation expressing its individuality and the freedom to make its own choices or the older generation wondering why the kids can't find value in the same virtues that it did. This pattern is repeated with every generation and it is likely a bit of both.

The differing behaviors that the various generations adopt have the potential to set up interesting situations within the work environment. One generation may expect that certain behaviors be deemed acceptable or even necessary within the working environment, behavior that another generation might find unacceptable or unrealistic. One has to be very careful though not to paint with a broad brush and to characterize a generation in a certain way without regard to individual differences. After all, generations are made up of individuals who are free to express their thoughts and behaviors as they desire. You are likely to find more variation of expression and behavior within one generation than you would across generations. General statements about what a generation is looking for over another are often nothing more than marketing contrivances. However, you will also find an interesting thing when you scratch a bit below the surface of some of the more obvious characteristics expressed as generational differences—great similarity, especially when it comes to the world of work.

The current school year is just about finishing up and the next generation of kids is searching for employment, for many of them their first real job. What new attitudes will they bring with them into the workplace and how will those attitudes affect their ability to succeed and interact successfully with the previous generations? Ron Zemke, along with his co-authors, captured in a book called "Generations at Work," a listing of water cooler conversations of what one generation might be saying about another. Here are some examples of the statements he captured:

- *They have no work ethic. They are just a bunch of slackers.*
- *So I told my boss, "If you are looking for loyalty, buy a dog."*
- *A hiring bonus! Wet behind the ears and he wants a hiring bonus! At his age, I was grateful to have a job!*

- *I have a new rule. I will not attend meetings that start after 5pm. I have a life.*
- *He asks me, "Do you have an email address?" I felt like telling him "Since you were in diapers buddy!"*
- *If I hear, "We tried that in '87' one more time, I'll hurl in his wrinkly old face."*

These statements give rise to the idea that there are vast differences between generations in the work place. One has to wonder that since every older generation seems to see risk in the behaviors and attitudes of every younger generation whether that "vision of peril" is, in fact, wired into who we are as a species. Does it help our survival as a species for each younger generation to rebel in its own fashion and to try new things? Does that behavior increase our adaptability as a species, allowing the younger generation to deal with new unexpected situations that might arise? Does it demarcate or set up conditions to prepare the younger generation and instill the ability to separate from their parents, to live independently? While some of us may consider our kids to be some new form of human, as we gaze into their rooms and review their behavior, they are just as human as you and I are. In addition, they carry the same psychological makeup that you and I do. So where do these differences come from?

Common statements that you hear today indicate that this "younger" generation cares less about job security and expects promotions faster than previous ones, among other differing expectations. Why might this younger generation care less about job security? I have asked this question many times. I usually get a variety of answers, but then I probe. Did we evolve somehow into another form of human from the previous generation that cared greatly about job security, to this generation that doesn't care? Did our psychological make-up somehow change? What caused this generation to care less?

Let's examine what employment conditions were like when this younger generation grew up. In general, the new generation grew up during a period of remarkably low unemployment. For example, according to the Bureau of Labor Statistics, in New York, the state where I graduated from high school and college, the historical high for unemployment was 10.5% in 1976, the year I was a junior in high school. The historical low was 4% in 1988 and today (March 2008) it is 4.8%. I can clearly remember a professor telling me to go to graduate school since there were no jobs currently available. And, I can remember when I was hiring employees in the late 80s to the late 90s, there were more jobs available then there were people to fill them.

If there were two or three opportunities for each person looking for a new job, might there be less concern about job security on the part of the worker? Might long-term loyalty be less important to them? I believe that the differing attitudes observed regarding unemployment between the various generations are largely due to the environment, in this case economic opportunity, rather than any fundamental differences. Further, I believe that if the younger generation experiences economic conditions similar to "my" generation, job security would be just as important to them as it was to me. Our generational differences were driven in large part by economic opportunity differences, and some other differences experienced in the environment in which we were raised. Given the same environmental conditions, each generation will make the same choices; we are after all, human.

When you take an attitudinal outcome measure regarding the workplace, say pride, satisfaction or engagement, and examine the drivers of those measures for generational differences, there will be some differences, but what you will be struck by is the far greater amount of similarity. (Drivers are areas of importance that move in tandem with an outcome measure. As the driver moves in the positive direction the outcome, say pride, moves in the positive direction as well. Strong drivers are those that most closely match the movements of the outcome variable). These differences can be explained as environmental variables, things that occur sometimes and not others, such as high or low amounts of unemployment. These are due to changes in the environment in which people live rather than due to differences in who people fundamentally are. You will find differences in the absolute scores regarding how positively one aspect of the workplace is viewed or not, but you will find much fewer differences in the drivers, especially those drivers that are fundamental.

Fundamental drivers are those that while they may be expressed differently in the day-to-day, are constant underneath. For instance, I would defy you to find any worker, from any generation, who did not want to be treated with respect and dignity at work. Their perceptions (the absolute score) and experiences will vary, but the desired end state, the state that will create a positively perceived environment for the employee, being treated with respect and dignity does not change. The organizational goal should be to create the conditions that allow each worker to feel that s/he is treated with respect and dignity. The range of conditions needed to accomplish that may differ, but not the desired end state. Other fundamental drivers include:

- A sense of fairness and equity (that for the effort expended there is a commensurate reward)
- Accomplishment (that what they are doing is meaningful)
- Trust in the organization (the organization and its management do what they say)
- Future (that there are compelling reasons to stick around)

- Effectiveness (that the organization provides what is needed to get the job done)
- Vision (that the work of the organization itself is important and the workers role in accomplishing that is clear)

As humans, we all are similar and we are all unique when it comes to the world of work. Our uniqueness allows for individual differences to emerge, but our uniqueness is not due to contrivances of generation, ethnicity, or even gender, but by experiences that those generations, ethnicities and genders experience.

The First Second

WEDNESDAY, MAY 14, 2007

ORGANIZATIONS

What makes an organization viable for human life? Do a small number of organizational variables, which have to be within acceptable range for an organization to support life, exist? If they do, when are the values of those variables set? And, once set, can they be changed?

> *"Everything should be made as simple as possible but no simpler."*
> *—Albert Einstein (1879-1955)*

The universe does not have to be the way it is. There are a small number of variables that, if their values had come out differently, we would not be here and life as we know it, would not be possible. Life exists in the universe because there are values in place for certain fundamental constants that allow matter to achieve high levels of organization. This led to the creation of stars and galaxies and other structures that permeate the universe. Other variables allow for stars to burn at a rate that keeps them around long enough for life to develop, and for carbon, what we know life to be based upon, to be found in abundance. Life and our universe are interconnected, but it did not need to be that way—the values of the constants did not need to be exactly as they are.

Why are they so? The simple answer is because we are here to measure it. There could have been an infinite number of universes before ours and there could be an infinite number of universes after ours is done. According to M-theory, there could be an infinite number of parallel universes to ours currently in existence. The reason why we are in possibly the one universe that supports life is because we are here in the first place to ask the question, and we would not be able to ask the question in any other universe that did not support life—this notion is called Anthropic principles.

"Nature does nothing in vain, and more is in vain when less will serve."
–Sir Isaac Newton (1642-1727)

The constants, the values that those critical variables adopted were determined within the first fraction of a fraction of a second that this universe existed. At the very beginning of our time, in our universe, a course was set. This course determined whether the possibility existed that we would be here now. If the numbers had not come out the way they did, I would not be sitting here writing this and you would not be reading it. In fact, there would in all likelihood be no life anywhere in this universe. The moment of origination was critical.

"Behind it all is surely an idea so simple, so beautiful, that when we grasp it—
in a decade, a century or a millennium—we will all say to each other, how could
it have been otherwise? How could we have been so stupid for so long?"
–John Archibald Wheeler (1911-2008)

What about organizational life? Can we draw a parallel to life in the universe or are humans and our societies more complex than the universe? Do relatively small numbers of variables or factors exist that create conditions within an organization, allowing employees to flourish, possibly according to Maslow to self-actualize? And when do these variables become part of the fabric of the organizational universe?

Each organization has a unique history, a unique story about its origins. Within a fairly short time span of its origins, the initial culture of the organization may be set, not necessarily in stone, but in fairly strong stuff nevertheless. I am constantly amazed at how in high turnover organizations, the cultures can be as robust as they are, resistant to movement in one direction or the other, even though they constantly fill with new people.

If you asked me to define the initial variables that determine whether an organization can support life, I would choose the following:

- A clear and compelling message regarding what the organization is about, what it stands for, what it hopes to accomplish and the knowledge of how each individual can support that message in a meaningful fashion
- Performance enablement—the organization providing what you need to accomplish your tasks in a way you can be proud and alignment of the performance expectations to the message
- Working for a management team that is effective and puts sensible business processes in place and positions itself well within its markets
- A sense of future—compelling reasons to stick around including:
  - Fair and respectful treatment—you get out what you consider to be fair for what you put in, covering pay, benefits, recognition, rewards and advancement as well as being treated in a respectful and dignified fashion
  - The ability to stay current in your skills or to develop new skills

The leadership of an organization needs to make up its mind regarding how they will operate against these variables during the initial formulation of the organization. While I do believe these variables can change, they are much more difficult to change later on in the organizational lifecycle than if they are set up appropriately at the beginning. The moment of origination is critical.

"What can be done with fewer assumptions is done in vain with more."
—William of Ockham (1285-1349)

THE NEXT 1000 YEARS

SATURDAY, MAY 17, 2008

ORGANIZATIONS

I was on a business trip in Italy when my driver indicated that we were traveling along the Appian Way. I was a bit stunned. Here I was on a business trip, where you typically see the airport, the inside of a taxi, a hotel and a meeting room, all accouterments of the modern world, and I was cruising in a car on a road that was more than 2000 years old.

I asked the driver to stop the car, and I got out and touched the road. Majestic old trees lined both sides of the cobblestone road, which was straight as an arrow, and as we made our way along, I got chills thinking about the Roman Legions, perhaps, marching along the very road I now traversed. This roadway helped Rome become an empire. Infrastructure matters, especially when it is a game changer—no one else had roadways like the Romans, allowing them to achieve things that others could not.

Let's do a thought exercise. If you knew you were going to live for 1000 years, what would you do differently? Today, we all seem to operate with a short time horizon. I am thrilled if I get 10 years out of a car, while others itch for a new one after three or five years. How would you feel if you knew you would be driving for the better part of 1000 years? What would you demand in a car? Does the Buick Century all of a sudden become more attractive; perhaps the

Millennium series of various Dodge vehicles excites you, or would you only shop the Infinity brand?

How would you educate yourself? I could take my time getting through college, say 50 years, and finally figure out calculus. It would probably take me 50 years, but then, maybe new avenues would open to me. A Ph.D. would become the equivalent of a high school diploma, at best, and a new higher standard of academic excellence would need to be achieved. (A new variation on an old joke: What do you call someone with a master's degree? The answer is, "a dropout.")

What would you look for in a house or other dwelling? Only a 20-year guarantee on that roof? Can I get a roof with a 200-year guarantee? After all, I don't want to constantly be replacing the roof; I need something a little more durable. If your time horizon were 1000 years, how would you handle issues that are relatively rare today?

For instance, you may experience a 100-year storm 10 times in your 1000-year lifetime that is devastating to homes and buildings in its path, buildings that are not built to last 1000 years. What about economic cycles or long-term development, research or construction projects? How about natural resources? What natural resources are we using today that are sustainable over 1000 year's time?

Why do you think banks are usually built out of bricks and stone, or with strong looking cement or marble columns? The bank wants to give the impression of longevity—that they will be around for 1000 years. How would you feel about going into a bank branch located in a trailer to deposit your hard-earned money? This might make you hesitate. Interesting things happen within a long-term time horizon. For instance, if you deposited $1000 in a CD at three percent interest, it would be worth $6,874,240,231,169,627 at maturity. That is six, almost seven quadrillion—and represents a lot of money. But in 1000 years, a quadrillion might not buy what it used to. Just to keep up with inflation at 3.01 percent during those 1000 years, you would need $7,575,079,084,827,028. In other words, .01 percent inflation above your interest rate would put you almost one quadrillion dollars down in purchasing power. What a bummer.

What about relationships? Would you behave any differently if you knew that the argument you just had might linger for 1000 years? Would we not get into as many arguments or would they just last longer? A mother might say, "Johnny, go to your room and don't come out until you are prepared to be civil to your sister." Five years later…Would we still enter into marriage or would some new form of relationship between men and women emerge? The average marriage today is said to last about seven years and 50 percent of all marriages end in divorce. Daunting numbers if you might be around for 1000 years. Say you held off and didn't get married until you were 100 years old, with an average marriage lasting seven years, you would get married around 128 times. While there are a few celebrities who approach that number, for most of us, something would have to change.

It seems like our time horizons are getting shorter and shorter and that impacts our organizations and our careers. Today, public companies are focused upon making next quarter's goals, a three-month time horizon, and those that do not are severely punished in the marketplace. Today's marketplace doesn't reward organizations for taking a long-term view.

Take a step back for a moment and consider a very long-term view. How would you build a company if you wanted it to last for 1000 years? What would you do differently? How would it be structured?

What emphasis would you place on product development and research, on sales and marketing, on quality and on maintaining its reputation? How would you recruit? What personnel policies and practices would you put into place? What competencies must the organization develop that would make it enduring? What would be sacred, unchanging during the life span of the organization and what would be malleable? And how much sense would it make to focus on the next quarter if you were aiming for a 1000-year time horizon?

There was an interview in a documentary about the construction of The Large Hadron Collider at CERN that sticks in my mind. CERN is part of the European Organization for Nuclear Research. The Large Hadron Collider is a new piece of equipment coming online and represents the culmination of a 13-year design and construction process and an engineering tour-de-force that has pushed the state-of-the art to the limit. The Large Hadron Collider will allow physicists to go where they have never been able to go before and to test out theories on the fundamental make-up of the universe. A construction engineer who was involved in building the Large Hadron Collider was being interviewed, and in the project construction reviews, he indicated that he is continually asked, "What unforeseen events or obstacles have you been able to foresee?" You could literally see his blood pressure rise as he considered it clear lunacy to ask how he has foreseen the unforeseen. If you were building an organization with a 1000-year time horizon, while you might not be able to foresee the unforeseen, your organization certainly needs to be able to handle the unforeseen. How would you build that in?

James Collins and Jerry Porras wrote "Built to Last," a bestselling book about what makes companies endure for the long term. But more than endure, what makes them standout leaders in their respective industries? They suggest a company develop core values, things that hold true for the long term. Around those core values, organizations should learn how to change the things that need to be adaptable to changing market conditions. They matched up companies they felt were truly outstanding organizations against those that they viewed as second tier. It is interesting to note that a number of companies they viewed as outstanding, while still successful by most measures, have recently fallen upon harder times. These include companies such as Ford, Citicorp, HP and IBM. Did they lose their vision, their core? What caused the decline? Maybe they could do a follow-up book on how outstanding companies lose their way. It reminds me a bit of the splash that the service profit chain at Sears made when it hit the *Harvard Business Review*. While it represents a lot of very good work, the approach did not prevent Sears from almost going belly-up. The fundamentals need to be in place, and the organization needs to be able to cope with changing market conditions in addition to holding onto its core—its essence.

So, what if you were building your organization to last for 1000 years? Would you do anything different? If you were to live for 1000 years, would you do anything different? And I think, most importantly, would we derive any shorter-term benefit by thinking in longer-term horizons? Maybe I should tackle calculus one more time.

...AND THE PURSUIT OF HAPPINESS

WEDNESDAY, JUNE 11, 2008

AROUND THE WORLD

"CPR kit available upon request" was written in black ink on
the somewhat small white, framed sign near the front door of a
Manhattan restaurant where I was having a business lunch. The
wording made me smile, specifically the words "upon request."
A picture formed in my mind of me clutching my chest, and as
I sank to the floor losing consciousness with no assistance, the
hostess explains to the other patrons waiting in line, "if only he had
requested the CPR kit before he lost consciousness, oh well…table
for two?" I began to think, that there are some things in life you
really shouldn't have to ask for—things that should be…inalienable.

The next day there was a cartoon in the paper that showed a flight
attendant giving the standard speech at the beginning of a flight. It
indicated that if a sudden decompression happened, an oxygen mask
would fall from the ceiling and for an additional $15, you could have
it activated.

I wondered if that could be paid in advance or whether you should
wait to see if you really needed it, in which case you could just pass
the money to the flight attendant and have it turned on. And I am
sure correct change would be appreciated in order to expedite things.

What makes the cartoon funny though, at least to me, is the
notion that you have to pay extra for something that you shouldn't

have to ask for, namely supplemental oxygen if you find yourself unexpectedly on a plane with a limited supply. Don't you just hate it when that happens? (The cartoon was poking fun at a U.S. airline that now charges $15 extra to bring a bag along on your trip. Who in their right mind would bring a bag packed with clothes or other essentials on a vacation or a business trip? So, given the unusual nature of people traveling with a suitcase, I can see the justification for charging extra for a piece of luggage instead of building the cost into the ticket itself.)

Thomas Jefferson, in writing the United States Declaration of Independence, listed "Life, Liberty and the Pursuit of Happiness" as the inalienable rights of mankind—supposedly things you shouldn't have to ask for, things that are guaranteed and cannot be taken away. (It says nothing about CPR kits or airline luggage, however, but perhaps he did not fly much). This phrase has shown up in a number of Supreme Court cases aimed at defining just what is covered by that broad statement. For instance, Chief Justice Earl Warren wrote in a 1967 ruling that helped to define the *Pursuit of Happiness*, "The freedom to marry has long been recognized as one of the vital personal rights essential to the orderly pursuit of happiness by free men." That judicial rendering was given to protect the rights of people from differing races to intermarry, and that same logic is beginning to be applied to people desiring same sex marriages, given their inalienable right to "the Pursuit of Happiness."

Many other documents carve out other inalienable rights such as "no one ought to harm another in his life, health, liberty or possessions" (John Locke). In the "Rights of Man," Thomas Paine wrote in 1791 regarding the equality of all men and their right to liberty. He stated that these rights should not be codified or put into legislation because that would imply that these rights are privileges that could be granted by legislation but then also taken away by legislation. Early Islamic law held much the same viewpoint (and may have influenced Paine) with fundamental rights of man existing that no ruler could put aside covering social, cultural, political, economic and civic rights. The concepts also included room for an independent judiciary that was not to discriminate against those appearing before it based on "religion, race, color, kinship or prejudice." These were inalienable rights with all that implied.

Alienable rights though are rights that are given either legislatively or through the grace of someone in power and can easily be taken away. Do employees have any inalienable rights? What about customers? In order to make a stab at answering those questions I would like to propose several concepts.

The first concept is that the difference between inalienable and alienable rights is a by-product of the times in which we live. We choose to make certain rights inalienable. The inalienable rights we enjoy in the U.S. in the twenty-first century look nothing like the inalienable rights enjoyed by some living in other parts of the world or by those from different periods. Inalienable rights if they were truly inalienable would be universally recognized by mankind rather than rights that needed to be secured, sometimes using force. "Life, Liberty and the Pursuit of Happiness," are those inalienable rights, or are they rights that those living today have decided to call inalienable? They are certainly noble and it makes you feel good to say that all mankind has certain inalienable rights, but I would suggest that we are a product and inalienable rights are a product of our times. Certainly there have been times, including right now, where Life, Liberty and the Pursuit of Happiness are not a given for a significant portion of the world's population, as much as we might think that they should be. Inalienable rights are a product of paradigm, precedent and principle, but sometimes, as with the Declaration of Independence, people are able to stand up and say it is time to change the paradigm.

The second concept is the notion that Darwin's principles of evolution can be applied to organizations as well as to living organisms. When organizations express *variation*, employees and customers have the ability to *select* the most appropriate organizations for them, the ones they want to work for, or be customers of, and the most robust organizations, the *fittest* (those that attract employees and customers for the long-term) will be the ones to *survive*. Other organizations, with their desire to survive as well, will copy the ideas and strategies of those organizations that they believe are being successful and hence those ideas, practices and procedures will be passed along to other organizations not through heredity, but by the spread of ideas—some would call them memes. Organizations have the right to deliver products and services as they see fit and customers have the right to utilize or not utilize that organization's products and/or services.

Those of us currently living in the U.S. have the tremendous good fortune of living in the wealthiest, most successful country that has ever existed. You could easily make the argument that no one living in the U.S. should be hungry, living on the street or be denied access to medical care—that food, shelter and medical care are inalienable rights. After all, are we so barbaric that we would step over homeless, hungry people sleeping on the street, likely in need of medical attention, as though they were somehow less than human? I have and it is very likely that a large number of those reading this probably have, too. It makes us uncomfortable and we are wary of the potential danger to ourselves, so we hesitate to reach out to those in need. How much better would you feel if you had a mechanism to help those you see living on the street? But for those living on the street, is it an inalienable right that they should expect that help? Let's explore one topic, healthcare, a little more closely for a possible answer.

Healthcare, which some purchase through their employer as a shared expense, does not have a lengthy history. It was only very recently that this expense became shared and not borne solely by the employer. But it was also not that long ago that it did not exist at all. Prior to WWII, healthcare was a rare commodity and became prevalent only as a way for employers to compete for hard-to-find employees. They provided healthcare insurance in order to increase the likelihood of their survival.

> During World War II, wage and price controls prevented employers from using wages to compete for scarce labor. Under the 1942 Stabilization Act, Congress limited the wage increases that could be offered by firms, but permitted the adoption of employee insurance plans. In this way, health benefit packages offered one means of securing workers... Under the 1954 Internal Revenue Code (IRC), employer contributions to employee health plans were exempt from employee taxable income. As a result of this tax-advantaged form of compensation, the demand for health insurance further increased throughout the 1950s, (Thomasson, 2003).

Therefore, employer-provided healthcare insurance, with the expense borne solely by the employer, really only existed from the mid-1940s to the 1990s, and now, most organizations require employees to share the cost. But does that mean that medical care is not an inalienable right?

Broadly speaking, the inalienable rights of employees consist of those things that either the organization must offer to remain viable (to attract employees), or that our society deems as basic. If society deems that universal health coverage is an inalienable right and that notion is broadly accepted, then that is what it becomes. Other rights that could be deemed as inalienable might include employment at will, a two-way street, benefiting both the employer and the employee, the ability to actually work at your trade (another Supreme Court definition of "the Pursuit of Happiness") and to not be restrained in your trade.

Broadly, it would seem that the one truly inalienable right that employees have is the right to choose whether they stay with their current employer. The rights you want to characterize as inalienable are only so when people are willing to stand up for them, to create a paradigm that says they are in fact inalienable. When employees and customers exercise their options by utilizing or being employed by organizations of their choice, they are creating the inalienable rights—rights that become part of the fabric of how business is conducted.

Organizations will sometimes conduct themselves in such a manner that leads the casual observer to question their viability. I was at LaGuardia about to board a flight when the woman in front of me, who was returning home, was asked to put her bag into the metal frame to see if it would fit and be allowed on the plane. She did, it didn't and she was told she would have to gate-check her bag. When she told the gate agent that she was allowed to bring the bag on the plane on the way to LaGuardia from Minneapolis, the response was "they cared less about those things in Minneapolis than in NYC." She was predictably upset. Does she have an inalienable right to expect consistency in standards applied within one airline from airport to airport? Only if she and all those affected by arbitrarily applied rules demand it. She needs to vote with her feet and fly another airline on her next trip. In a non-perfect world, however, we do not have completely free choice, as sometimes our options can be limited.

With respect to safety, I would think that customers would have the reasonable expectation that certain practices and procedures to ensure their safety would be followed when they engage with organizations in activities that carry with it a certain amount of risk, such as flying in an airplane. But I don't think that rises to the level of inalienable rights. Airlines will practice safe procedures either because they need to in order to comply with legislation and be allowed to keep flying, or because if they get a reputation as an unsafe airline, no one is going to use them. Restaurants will operate with cleanliness for the same reasons—legislative necessity or reputation and on and on.

There are some things in life you shouldn't have to ask for, but they occur not because we have naturally given inalienable rights simply because we are human, but because we choose to live our lives in such a fashion and to conduct ourselves toward others that these rights can be inferred. And while these rights may change over the ages, and depending on which political system you live within, one thing does seem certain, each of us will determine that the inalienable rights generally acknowledged do exist. But I still would prefer not having to specifically ask for the CPR kit prior to passing out.

Personal aside: At this time, in this place I would argue, and I think our society's standards would argue that access to medical care, in whatever form, is in fact an inalienable right and that there should be no employee—in fact no person—in the U.S. without access to care. But the reason for that is not that it has to be. The reason for that is that given what we are now capable of as a country, as a society, it is not only right that it should be, but that it is in our own best interests to ensure that the people who live within our borders have access to healthcare.

LABOR RELATIONS

THURSDAY, JUNE 19, 2008

HUMAN RESOURCES

Have you ever seen a worker walking a picket line with a sign saying, "Give me more challenging work?" I am quite sure I never have. The signs they carry on the picket lines tend to say things like, "Better pay," "No layoffs," "We want health insurance," "Don't treat us like animals," etc. So, what causes people to seek third party representation? Using employee surveys, how would you build a warning indicator that gives the organization a wake-up call, that unless it takes corrective action, it is on a path that will lead to its employees to organize?

Without passing judgment on whether unions are positive or negative, there are conditions that when present, lead workers to seek third party representation in the form of unions. (For our purposes here, I will deal only with voluntary unions, where workers have an option to create and/or join a union. I will not be dealing with mandated or legislated unions that exist in some countries.) Very broadly, when workers are dissatisfied about certain aspects of their jobs and feel powerless to do anything about them, they are vulnerable to organizing attempts. When workers feel pleased about the working conditions and their treatment at work, they are less vulnerable to organizing.

People who have joined unions will often report these reasons as to why they joined:

- Higher wages and more influence in the wage-setting process
- Increased job security
- Improved benefits (insurance, pensions, personal and sick time, vacations, work breaks etc.)
- Improved working conditions (physical conditions, safety, work pace, etc.)
- Clearer, fairer rules for job transfers, discipline, promotion and grievances
- Greater self-control in the workplace

Specifically, one study that was conducted regarding the propensity to vote for union representation (voting the union in) revealed the following dimensions were the strongest predictors of the election outcome. These are the dimensions that when workers are most displeased about the likelihood of them, seeking third party representation is greatest—hence the negative correlations.

DIMENSION	r
Job Security	-.42
Wages	-.40
Overall Satisfaction	-.36
Treatment Satisfaction	-.34
Benefits	-.31
Recognition	-.30
Promotions	-.30

(N=1000, .99 level of confidence)

Unions have existed for a long time and they have been fighting for what they believe their members want. In general, unions have negotiated wages, benefits and other working conditions and have increased the level of those attributes for their members (i.e. union members on average are paid more than non-members doing similar work). Do those increased levels have an effect on employee attitudes? Yes they do. Union members are, in general, more positive about things like pay and benefits, things that unions have been fighting for since their inception.

Based on the information we have reviewed so far, it would seem that a "labor relations" or "unionization" index would need to cover the following topics or areas to be as good of a warning indicator as possible:

- Pay
- Benefits
- Job Security
- Grievances
- Supervision
- Safety, Physical Working Conditions
- Resources to do Job

- Overall Satisfaction
- Job Satisfaction
- Pride
- Respectful Treatment
- Well-Being
- Trust in Leadership
- Recognition

Hence, survey items to be used in a labor relations index could include:

- Overall, I am satisfied with my organization as a place to work.
- I am proud to work for my organization.
- I am paid fairly for the work I do.
- I am satisfied with the benefits I receive at this company.
- I currently feel confident that I will not be laid off from my job.
- Any complaints I have are heard fairly by the organization.
- My ideas and opinions count.
- My manager is a good supervisor, competent technically and from a human relations perspective.

- I trust the leadership of this company.
- I have the tools and equipment I need to do my job effectively.
- This is physically a safe place to work.
- Physical working conditions (space, lighting, noise, etc.) are good where I work.
- I enjoy my work, it is satisfying.
- My manager treats me with respect.
- My manager cares about my well-being.
- I receive appropriate recognition for the work I do.

These items (some may use slightly more, some slightly fewer) cover topics that have been shown to be related to labor relations or unionization and can be averaged together to form an index that creates an indicator of a deteriorating labor relations climate. Once the index has been created and data have been collected, how do you know at which score to intervene?

For warning indicators, the question becomes one of defining the trigger point at which an intervention should be mounted. If the percent favorable is 50%, does that trigger a warning? What about 65%? Do varying trigger points result in differing actions? A 50% favorable score may yield a closer follow-up and a 40% favorable score yields an all-hands-on-deck intervention? You can set your trigger points either higher or lower depending on the certainty needed, when determining if a location may be having labor relations issues. You can also set differing actions to kick in at varying trigger points.

Wohlman's Union Problem

Wednesday, August 6, 2008

Human Resources

By 1896, Abraham Wohlman, who was getting on in years, was a relatively wealthy man. Originally from Bialystok, he was living in Belz, Bessarabia. He owned a bookbinding shop and did enough volume that he was able to employ 10 workers year-round. In addition to his bookbinding shop, he also owned a bookstore from which he sold textbooks and school supplies. He was very lucky to hold a contract with the local school system providing them with school supplies covering the elementary schools to the upper grades of the gymnasia, equivalent to a U.S. high school today. In the late 1800s, Belz, not one of the main population centers in Bessarabia, had no university.

Though he was living with the hardships and restrictions associated with Czarist Russia, Abraham Wohlman lived a fine life. Married, with three children (two boys and a girl), he was a very warm and compassionate fellow, who was well respected by and a supporter of his community. He had a nice house located on a side street in town, with a yard large enough to keep three to four cows, chickens, geese, ducks, and grow vegetables. He provided jobs to others in the community and treated his workers as extensions of his own family, providing them with wholesome meals at his family's table that they all shared together. When he wanted his two grandchildren to take language lessons, Abraham Wohlman hired a tutor named Benjamin Saltzman, my great-grandfather, to provide private lessons at his house.

A new worker at Wohlman's, one who had served an apprenticeship as a bookbinder (which was started as young as 11 years of age), but still early career as a craftsman, would make about 8 rubles a month or 96 rubles a year. For some context, a small three room cottage with dirt floors cost about 400 rubles. Each worker at Wohlman's had the right to join any political party, and a great diversity of political thought among the 10 workers occurred, each assuming that their choice was the best and trying to convince the others to see things their way. It was a dynamic, thoughtful environment. But for a worker, life was hard and economically, in general, people were not well off as they struggled to put food on their tables and to survive. Benjamin Saltzman had moved his family to Belz from Brateslav and after working as a tutor for a number of years, bought a house on the Klezmershe Gesl or street of the musicians (each trade had it own street name) and opened a small grocery store. The store had dirt floors and it was not unusual for thieves to dig under the walls of the store to steal food, for they were hungry—times were tough for many.

A writer describes a first person account of the street in the spring:

> The frost subsided and the ice began to melt. And the lovely warm spring sun likewise appeared in all its splendor and radiance. And even the Klezmershe Gesl became alive too, with all its mud and slush. It was impossible to cross the street even in the tallest boots. The mud swelled up so that it literally overflowed its boundaries onto the sidewalk, and it would not

take long for it to pour into the houses themselves. I think that no other town in Russia had such deep mud as was found in the Klezmershe Gesl in Belz. The mud had respect only for that person who had boots that reached up to his knees.

Fear increasingly entered the lives of the people of Belz. During April 6-7, 1903 the Kishinev Pogrom occurred (Kishinev is the capital of the Bessarabia Province where Belz is located). Forty-seven people were killed, 92 critically wounded, 500 injured and 700 homes looted or destroyed during rioting. Czarist authorities did nothing to prevent the attacks until the 3rd day. In October 1905, a second attack occurred with 19 killed and 56 injured. (Because of the first attack, self-defense organizations arose, which limited the number of deaths during the second). Those who were fearful for their safety reported that they "couldn't go to the police, for we didn'ttrust them."

In 1905, as conditions in Russia continued to worsen, union organizers came to Belz and convinced Wohlman's workers to join a union that they were setting up throughout the province. The union was pitched as a method by which the conditions of their lives, safety, security and standards could be improved.

> Our shop also became involved in "the movement." And six months later a strike was declared. To tell the truth, not every worker was pleased with the strike, because all those who worked for Wohlman respected him and even loved him. He treated the workers like his own children, and not like strangers.

The new union that the workers had joined concluded that it was not right for workers to eat their meals in the home of the Wohlman, to be "treated as his own children." Further, they felt that wages should be raised enough so that each worker could decide on their own where they would eat their meals. By treating the workers as "family," which included having them eat meals at Wohlman's family dinner table, and not paying them sufficiently for them to be independent of that somewhat feudal system, the union felt that the treatment the workers received held an element of disrespect. Wohlman who had welcomed each employee as family saw it differently and refused to accept such conditions under any circumstances. He was able to provide for his workers at a cost less than what he would have to pay them for the same ability, for he fed them partly out of the bounty of his homestead. Providing sufficient wages to each worker to take their meals independently would cost him a greater amount.

One worker in Wohlman's employ stated:

> I can safely vouch that the workers did not enjoy as good a home in their own houses as they did at Wohlman's. It was for this reason that he did not want to pay his workers for their food, since his house was filled with everything of the best, which cost him very little. And so the strike continued ever more stubbornly, so that it became impossible to reach an agreement.

> I realized that the strike will not end very soon while the workers were marching around Wohlman's house. Each striker had to find his own place to stay and a place to eat. I knew the difficult position of my family who, in their extremity, looked forward to my earnings from which even earlier I could not lay aside enough for their needs. And the union could give us no help at all. It simply had no money to pay out, for it had been organized only a short while before. I saw that if I stayed here longer I would soon be left without any money at all. This

was my greatest problem at the time. I was sure of one thing; when and if the strike were settled I would again get work at the Wohlman's, since he considered me his best worker and he liked me very much.

While the details of what caused Wohlman's union problem differ from the more common ones today, the underlying issues are absolutely the same. It would be unusual though not unheard of for workers today to take their meals with the owner's family as a way for the owner to save money on wages; however, the underlying issues that it highlights, respectful treatment, sense of equity, fairness surrounding pay, benefits, control over one's own destiny are very common causes of labor unrest. The uncertainty of the times with extreme violence breaking out, uncertainty about safety and security as well as poor treatment of the citizenry by those in authority, laid the foundations necessary for fertile union organizing. The strike at Wohlman's, with workers walking the picket lines, lasted approximately one year. It was then settled with the workers receiving enough of a wage increase that they could choose to eat their meals wherever they wanted. While the strikers did come back to work at Wohlman's bookbinding shop, what I don't know from the material available to me is whether they were ever welcomed back at Wohlman's dinner table.

VALUES AND ADDICTION

WEDNESDAY, JUNE 25, 2008

CURRENT EVENTS

Saltzman: *one who processed and sold salt.*

Salt used to be worth its weight in gold. In fact, before there was
gold as a valued metal, there was salt as a valued mineral. Up until
the 1900s, salt was difficult to obtain and given its importance in
sustaining life, it was quite prized. It is speculated that the rise and
fall of certain civilizations was impacted by their access to salt. The
word "salary" came from the Roman word "salarium" or salt money
and Rome's legionnaires were occasionally paid in salt. While the
locals may have been dubious about the value of a Roman coin
backed by a far away government, or by a lack of enough coins
in circulation to maintain a money-based economy, a soldier who
had salt had a valuable commodity that was easily traded for other
goods and services. And in periods of uncertainty, salt was better
than coinage for its value was clear to everyone. Too much salt
though causes problems. For instance, salt was used by the military
to gain control over others as far back as 4500 years ago. By salting
the fields of people you were at war with, you could prevent them
from growing crops. If you have too little salt, life becomes very
difficult, perhaps even leading to death. Having too much salt can
cause the same outcome, but the right amount of salt is a pleasure
as evidenced by humans evolving receptors on our tongues for

detecting and enjoying the taste of salt. Salt today is very common, one of the few bargains you can find at the grocery store and we now tend to over-salt our foods resulting in some long-term health issues. Salt moved from a rare material of very high worth to a commodity. Science and technology allowed that to happen.

Gold is another rare commodity that has served as a basis for monetary systems. But as opposed to salt, you can live without gold. The value of gold is completely dependent on what someone is willing to pay for it. In 1980, a troy ounce of gold was selling for about $641 dollars; by 2000, its price had fallen to $272. On June 19, 2008 on the spot market for gold, an ounce was selling for $903. People have recently turned to gold and hence have run up the price because of the perception of safety in gold holding its value better during uncertain times than other potential investments. However, gold has little to no-inherent value, other than its use in some manufacturing processes and products. Its true value lies in its desirability and the demand for it from other people, simply because it is rare and desired. (All the gold ever mined by humans would form a cube 19 meters on a side).

In my town, one way you can tell the age of a house is to look at its position relative to the road and its garage size. My town was founded in 1695, and while I don't think there are any houses left that go back that far, the oldest houses are those that are right up against the road with little to no driveway in front of the house. The reason for that is simple. Of the little traffic they had back then, when you pulled up to a house on your horse, you did not need to pull into a driveway. The next generation of houses had smallish driveways, but no garages; then came single then double and now most new houses are built with three car (or more) garages here. We live in a society that has become very energy dependent and automobile centric. Our road systems, our transport systems, most of our cities, the way we shop and travel to work, the way we build our homes are all centered around our use of the automobile as a means of transport. Our automobiles predominantly run on gas and our society as a whole is very oil dependent.

The price of oil is now a source of concern to many if not most. Heating our homes, running our cars, the costs of goods and services are all getting more expensive due to the added energy costs in producing those products and services. Oil, and energy historically, has been a commodity, one that has been more or less reasonably priced here in the U.S. In the recent past, many would think nothing of filling up the tank on a nice Saturday and going for a ride in the country. People now think twice about what filling that tank will cost. I am certainly not the first to say it, but as a society, we are addicted to oil, and historically the reasonable price has exacerbated that addiction. We are still addicted to oil, but now the oil is getting very expensive and will likely push higher. Debates go on about why that is happening. Is it the oil companies, the countries with the oil resources, the refineries, or oil speculators, the hedge funds, the declining value of the dollar?

Oil has been referred to as black gold. (Was it Jedd Clampet who originally called it "Texas tea"?) Rather than a comparison to gold, oil though is more like salt. Today, our society is so dependent on oil, given the way we are structured, that we literally cannot continue as a society without it. So in uncertain times what is oil worth? What should it be worth? What is it worth to keep our society functioning in the much same manner to which we are familiar? While I am feeling as much pain as the next guy when I have to fill up my gas tank or home heating oil tank, I could not help but think about what may be happening in the manufacturing sector now that the price of oil is as high as it is. Friday, June 13, 2008, appearing in the *Wall Street Journal* was a story that started, "The rising cost of shipping everything from industrial pump parts to lawn-mower batteries to living-room sofas is forcing some manufacturers to bring production back to North America and freeze plans to send even more work overseas."

If you think of raw materials, infrastructure, workers' wages, transportation and the local business climate (taxes, etc.) as all components of the total cost of a product, oil may not be all that is inappropriately priced at the moment. For it seems that we are reaching a point of balance whereby given the total cost of producing a product, it is beginning to look attractive again to bring manufacturing back to the U.S., given the high cost of transport. The current price of oil and, hence, the transportation costs of goods is offsetting the lower wages paid elsewhere. At the current oil price, the incentive to move manufacturing outside of the U.S. is disappearing. So while we are facing pain at the pump, every time we fill our tanks, at this price point, are we now paying a price that will eventually bring manufacturing jobs back to these shores? Can we actually be heading down a path that will create local manufacturing jobs by paying these insane prices? But we are not the only ones paying these high prices. Those located in low wage countries (those where the cost of oil is not subsidized) are paying higher prices as well. How much greater is the pain for them? How will it end? As in the cold war, the answer may be which society can outspend the other prior to collapse.

At the current price point for oil, there certainly seem to be incentives for entrepreneurs to develop energy alternatives to oil. And any discomfort that the oil producing nations are currently feeling has nothing to do with the current price of oil per se, but that at the current price we have reached a point where alternatives to oil

Energy will be developed, potentially causing the long-term value of

energy will be developed, potentially causing the long-term value of oil to plummet. At the current pain level, we just might decide that it is time to kick the addiction. Remember what happened to the value of salt, a once hard to find commodity.

The percentage of high school seniors who report that they smoke cigarettes daily has dropped to just over 10 percent. And new work published May 22, 2008 in the *New England Journal of Medicine* suggested that those who decide to quit smoking are influenced by individuals from social networks with connections up to three degrees of separation (meaning a friend of a friend of a friend). Work done on the brain has recently shown that the same parts of the brain are used when remembering the past and attempting to envision the future. This would suggest that those kids who develop the ability to kick their addiction, influenced by their extended peer set and develop a past, a history of not smoking, will be more likely to envision a future for themselves where they do not smoke.

If we speculate that similar mechanisms may be at play in organizations, (since organizations are simply an amalgamation of people, most of whom attended 12th grade), it may be that once they develop alternative energy solutions to service their needs, perhaps influenced by those other organizations with whom they are only remotely connected, that a critical mass will begin to develop. Once we head down the path of alternative energy, once the momentum is built and new products and services that are not as dependent on oil are more commonplace, additional products and services will likely arise. The difficulty of seeing an alternative energy future, to envision what that future may be like, may ease once there is some alternative energy history in place, if not in the immediate organization itself then within peer network organizations. Envisioning the future is apparently more easily done when you can refer to the past, even perhaps if that past is not your own but from elsewhere within your network.

Other organizational behavior may be operating based on similar mechanisms. Why, over a very short period, did organizations move from a defined benefit employee retirement plan to a defined contribution? (Yes, they saved money and reduced risk exposure, but what made that course of action acceptable?) Once the trend began, and a little history developed, with few exceptions the rest moved in lockstep. Some now have even done away with any retirement contribution. Will the rest shortly follow? Why did organizations move to outsourcing, off shoring; why do they merge and reorganize the way they do? Could it perhaps be because of historical memory, perhaps even if it comes from other organizations? The likelihood of that greatly increases when you consider the way that people today shift from organization to organization carrying their organizational memories with them.

Too little oil can make life very difficult, but too much oil can cause an addiction to a predominantly single energy source, rather than a nice diverse basket of energy resources. We all know that the prudent course to take when investing is to diversify, to spread your risk around; yet we as an economy, as a society; were willing to place most of our eggs into the oil energy basket because it was economically attractive to do so. It is time for us to spread the risk around. Science and technology can make that happen. Just the right amount of oil, providing critical products that are hard to reproduce using alternatives, but also incenting alternative energy solutions would seem to be in our long-term best interest. Drilling in ANWAR on the north shore of Alaska or drilling off of our coasts has been described as giving the addict one more hit. It may provide very short-term relief (given the lead time in exploring, drilling and commercialization, the time until that relief might be measured in decades), but does nothing to get us past our addiction.

For the short-term, I will likely need to take out a loan every time I fill up the tank, but I can envision a future…

Organizational Civilization

Monday, July 7, 2008

Performance

Being civilized is commonly referred to as a high state of refinement. But what really matters, what allows us to call one place or culture civilized and another uncivilized? Can one organization be deemed as civilized while another is deemed as uncivilized?

I just got back from a vacation in the Adirondack Mountains, a Vermont-sized piece of real estate with a mix of public and private lands. In describing the accommodations available, the word *uneven* comes to mind. At one extreme, you can rent a private island on one of the spectacular lakes that along with luxurious "rustic" accommodations, comes complete with a chef, boathouse, boatman, guide and will set you back in the mid 5-figures for a week. At the other end of the spectrum, you can rent a cabin that does not have running water or electricity; it may or may not have a bowed roofline, which can cause anxious moments as you wonder if the roof will collapse around you while you sleep. Most people, as we did, rent something in between.

Our small cabin was built in the early 1900s. At some point, electricity was added as was running water. Later, a modernish bathroom was added off the front porch. In order to get to the bathroom, you had to pass through the front porch (and a few spider webs). Heat in the uninsulated cabin was provided by a fireplace and the windows served as the air-conditioner. The galley kitchen had appliances dating back to the 1940s and 1950s. At night, we used a sleeping porch, a common approach to sleeping in the mountains during the summer. It is essentially a screened outdoor porch with a bed. No television. No phone. No cell phone reception. No computer hookup or Wi-Fi. Isolated. Rustic. Uncivilized?

Our living room had a couch and a couple of chairs huddled around the fireplace. In one corner was a piano, which to my ear, was well tuned. In the adjacent corner, bookshelves were filled with all types of books (some likely left by previous renters as I found one to be a vile work of bigotry from the 1920s). In another corner was a writing desk for penning notes to those left at home with an inkwell and quill pen. (The nearest post office was about 20 miles away). A globe rested nearby on a pedestal and reflected some long ago country names such as Siam, Dutch East Indies and Persia.

The sleeping porch, in addition to the bed, had a table and rocking chairs scattered around. It had a screen door, which led to the outside and bounced shut as you let it go, no real barrier to any creature that wanted to get in. But at night, as you drifted off to sleep, you could hear the loons calling in the distance. In the morning, the alarm clock played, a chorus of gifted songbirds that seemed thrilled by the vision of the sun creeping over the edge of the lake. A few mornings the temperature dipped in the low 50s, giving a good reason to stay comfortably buried under the covers. But a steaming cup of tea or coffee made on the 1940s stove never tasted quite as good as when consumed in the chilly cabin, as the early morning sunlight began to stream through the windows.

In the afternoon, after a day of hiking or canoeing, we would travel about 10 miles or so to an ice cream shack that made a daily flavor.

A big sign hung over the counter, "The flavor of the day has already been decided. What size would you like?" We got a schedule of flavors that were going to be made each day we were there, and Wednesday morning my daughter and I woke up eager to go because it was chocolate day (my wife preferred "mystery fruit day"). Uncivilized?

Amid all these rustic surroundings, I started to speculate regarding the nature of civilized versus uncivilized organizations. What is the essence of an organization that will be successful? Does it have anything to do with its degree of refinement? Some organizations operate with a high degree of refinement, with rules and procedures in place, proper ways of doing things, forms to complete, approvals to be received, very buttoned up and proper.

Other organizations operate with a much simpler approach, maybe an old-fashioned approach to procedures and policy; maybe they could be characterized as slightly uneven in their approach to things, lacking refinement. But you also have to wonder what the refined organizations with their policies and procedures, buttoned up practices have lost.

Can they hear the call of the loons in the night through their sealed windows in their air-conditioned offices? As we unrelentingly move our lifestyles to be more comfortable with modern conveniences and choices, and as we move our organizations to adopt more sophisticated approaches to get things done, what do we lose? What do our organizations lose? Is there something to be gained by maintaining some of the old-fashioned approach to getting things done, while adopting the best of modern practices?

My Jeans are Irregulars

Wednesday, March 5, 2008

Performance

Stories are passed down through European families regarding what members of the family did to escape, avoid or deal with the horrors of WWII. One method I have read about describes how families struggled to obtain fake passports for use in their attempts to flee. There is a story that takes place in Poland in the late 1930s. The story describes how passports were forged by studying old passports from many different countries; their style and format were then copied creating new fake passports for those trying to escape.

One day a man, who was part of the underground, set out to collect old passports through whatever method he could. He was extremely successful and by the end of the day, he had collected a large number. On the way back from his activities, he was stopped by the Polish police, was asked for his papers and then confronted when they discovered the large number of passports he was carrying. He was sure that they would take him to the police station, torture and kill him as they tried to learn about the activities of the underground organization.

The man thought about how troubled his family would be if they never saw him again without any explanation. But, it was near the end of the day and the police told the man to go home and come to the station in the morning for questioning. The man was terrified. The police knew who he was and if he stayed home and did not show up the next day or if he tried to flee that night, they would simply go to his house and kill his family. If he showed up the next day at the police station, they would torture him to obtain information and then kill him anyway. He did not know what to do. After much deliberation and consultation, he went to the police station the next morning and approached the police officer who had stopped him. The police officer asked him what he wanted and appeared not to remember the previous day's incident. The man indicated that he had been stopped and a packet of passports had been taken from him and he was here to collect it. The police officer handed the man the packet of passports and told him to be on his way.

Saliency, as a psychological concept, deals with how central an event, object, fact or perception is to you or another person and may be the result of emotional, motivational or cognitive factors. To the man with the passports, being stopped by the police was extremely central to his very existence for it was quite literally life or death. To the police officer, the man was one of hundreds of people who he had stopped and questioned that day. The man with the passports described the incident as a miracle, that his and his family's lives were spared. From his perspective, it certainly was. But what was the underlying mechanism of human perception that allowed that miracle to occur? Saliency. To the police officer, the incident was not nearly as salient, not nearly as memorable as it was to the passport procurer.

I don't envy the Transportation Security Agency (TSA) officers who screen airport passengers, checking each one as they pass through metal detectors and x-ray their bags. They are faced with an unenviable task. They have to keep constant vigilance, maintaining the saliency of forbidden items in their consciousness as thousands of people pass in front of them in a steady stream. As thousands of objects and people pass through your consciousness each day, maintaining the saliency of every one, to eliminate errors that can creep in due to the repetitive nature of the work is difficult, and we read about how, when tested, objects that should not be getting through are, as their saliency decreases.

When you start a new job, the current employees have an easier time remembering who you are, for them, you are very salient, the new object in their environment. But for you, you need to remember a large number of new people, making the task of remembering any specific person that much more difficult—unless something about them is extremely salient.

I have to admit, not being all that concerned about fashion, I buy irregular jeans. I grew up wearing two pairs of jeans (one pair to wear while the other pair was being washed). I like to wear jeans. But I don't like what jeans cost these days. So I go to a manufacturer's outlet mall near my home and I buy irregular blue jeans. As I pull each pair off the shelf and examine them, I am usually hard pressed to determine why they are called irregular. I look for the obvious, for instance, does it have three legs? (Well I could always use a spare, in case I get a hole in one knee). I usually cannot find anything wrong with them. When I wear them, at least at first, I wonder if what is not obvious to me, the irregularities, are likely very obvious to those around me and I am sure I can hear people pointing at me and laughing as I walk by. However, maybe it is not the jeans that bring on the laughter. But in reality, no one is looking at my jeans, let alone looking for the defect in my irregulars. I just think they are, at least for a moment, because the issue is more salient to me. It is very much more salient to me that I am wearing irregulars, until I forget about it, but no one else cares. (Try using that logic on a teenager.)

When a manager makes an off-hand comment to a worker about that worker's performance or future, what may be perceived by the manager as a minor topic or issue, just above the threshold of consciousness, may be perceived quite differently by the employee. To the employee, that comment might be indicative of whether or not he/she has a future with the organization, central to his/her very existence, while the manager might not even remember the comment the next day. How many cases of miscommunication in the workplace are derived from a comment that has very different levels of saliency to the various people who might be listening to it? Managers may use what they perceive as throw away lines, about "future opportunities" or "earnings potential" not really thinking about just how closely the employee is listening or just how salient those messages might be to the listener.

Another example of a routine event taking on added saliency recently occurred in North Korea where the NY Philharmonic gave a performance. The final piece played was a traditional Korean folk song. At the conclusion of the piece, the audience gave a standing ovation. The audience and the performers began waving to each other, as though they were two ships passing in the night, ships that did not want the brief beacons of light shining from each ship and seen by the other to be extinguished. Those brief beacons held all sorts of messages that the audience and performers wanted to pass to each other but were unable to expand upon in that setting. It was palpable. Messages that were saying "we are people too, don't hate us" and "how can we get past the issues that our two countries face?" Anyone who saw that could not help but be moved and could easily realize the saliency of the performance to those in attendance; it was not just another performance.

Can a stimulus or event become salient to you if it is subliminal? The notion of something being "subliminal" is that it exists below the threshold at which you perceive it. There are some, however, that believe that a subliminal stimulus can actually effect behavior. I have to state that I am highly skeptical about this. If a stimulus is truly subliminal, and not perceived by the individual, it is hard to imagine how it can affect behavior. There was enough concern surrounding this, however, that in the 1970s, congressional hearings were held to probe the effects of subliminal advertising on the American population. If something can actually affect your perception, then by definition, it is not subliminal and your body in fact perceives it. Let's put hair splitting aside for a moment; could an event because of its differing saliency to different individuals be subliminal to one and very salient to another? Have you ever sat next to a passenger on a plane who was extremely upset about bumps occurring during the flight, bumps that a frequent traveler fails to even notice?

In the work environment, similar occasions can arise and being sensitive to the differing levels of saliency that an event can hold for different people can make you more sensitive to those around you. This sensitivity will translate into increased empathy (for most) and in the end better relations with those around you.

Words and Behavior

ABC

Friday, July 18, 2008

Organizations

How important are words? Do words have the power to shape
our thinking or are they nothing more than a reflection of what
our minds are processing, giving substance to existing abstractions
floating in our heads? That is the essence of a debate that has gone
on for more than 100 years. Think of the words we use to describe
numbers, *one, two, ten, fifty*. Are we naturally inclined to develop words
to describe numbers? Do the words themselves, the words that we
have made up to signify quantities give us the ability to think both
abstractly and concretely about numbers, or is the ability to think
numerically built into the structure of our brain? Said another way,
is the ability to think logically about quantities an inherent ability,
independent of language, and are the words we have developed
simply an expression of that ability, or do the words shape our ability
to think in a numerical sense?

There is a tribe from Brazil, the Pirahã, who have no word for the
number *one* or any other exact quantity. This is apparently the first
group ever studied that has no concept for the number one. A
new study demonstrates that the Pirahã can still convey quantity
somewhat, but are essentially using words that mean few, some and
more. Other researchers contend that the words they are using mean
one, two and many. In either case in the Pirahã society, the need for
being able to quantify things precisely and hence develop a language
system that allows for that, was not a cultural priority.

As strange as you might find a society without words for specific numbers, remember that the first evidence for the use of the concept of zero is from the Sumerians in Mesopotamia about 5000 years ago. From there it traveled to the Indus Valley, and was used in Hindu society. In the Indus Valley, it was picked up by Arab merchants, became very important in their trade, and spread throughout Arab society. The Greeks only occasionally used the concept and Romans had no concept of zero (for those of you who remember Roman numerals try writing zero). On the other side of the globe, the Mayans independently invented their own version of zero. The concept of zero slowly migrated around the world and did not make it into European society until the late middle ages. Europe was stubbornly holding on to the use of the Roman traditional counting system rather than adopting new methods. So while we take zero for granted today, it is a relatively new concept for western culture.

Do words shape our thinking? One urban legend states that Eskimos who live in snowy places, and hence deal with snow more regularly than most of us, have developed many more words than exist in English to describe types of snow. That is apparently not true. First, Eskimos are not a unitary people and of the many groups that consist of Eskimos, many different languages exist. Second, the language structure of these groups is different, allowing for combinations that do not exist in English, making comparisons between the numbers of words that exist to describe snow very difficult. They may or may not have a few more words than there are in English to describe snow, but it is certainly not hundreds as the urban legend claims.

There are words that have been consistently used to reinforce messages of hatred, words that need no repetition here. Those words tend to be used repeatedly to denigrate others within societies around the world. Does the constant use of words of hatred reinforce the pattern of biased and bigoted thinking within the minds of those who use them or are they simply an expression of what is already there? Clearly, some believe that words of hatred create beliefs and behaviors of hate, as there are schoolchildren in various locations who are learning the vocabulary of "hatred" and "to hate" as part of their daily lessons. But what happens to these children later on? Can they ever put the hatred aside once it becomes part of who they are, part of their essence? The future for the majority of children who grow up on hatred looks very bleak and greatly saddens me.

There is a raging debate going on about the vocabulary of rap music. Words that denigrate are built into the lyrics of certain performers. These words perpetuate negative stereotypes, but are rationalized as being ok since they are coming from within a community. I can't agree with this at all. I strongly believe in first amendment rights, but people should be aware of what they are doing and the implications of the choices they make. Words of hate will have hateful results—regardless of the source. Just as yelling "fire" in a crowded theater is not protected speech, yelling out hate filled words for mass distribution should not be protected speech as well.

Stringing together words of hate into sentences can produce what some would call jokes. Jokes made at the expense of others, jokes that denigrate others for being different or being perceived as a threat to those giving word to those statements of hatred, hatred couched in supposedly humorous terms.

Each organization also has a vocabulary, words that they use in their day-to-day operations. (I am not talking about acronyms.) How important are the words that are used in our organizations? They can't be less important than the impact that words have in our everyday lives and in our shared histories. Developing unique organizational vocabularies that allow for both abstract reasoning and concrete discussions on the issues critical to the organization's success may give an organization a competitive edge. Unique vocabularies, ways of expression may allow the organization to consider concepts and ways of working that competitors are unable to replicate. Words are important, they have power, they have impact, and they should be used with care. People when speaking for themselves need to choose their words with care. People when speaking on behalf of organizations need to choose their words with care as well.

Results Not Typical

Wednesday, July 23, 2008

Employee Research

"I got this body while eating pizza, hamburgers," and then she leans forward whispering into the camera "even chocolate!" As her before and after pictures are displayed, the shapely product promoter is explaining how she lost all that weight and became irresistible by eating the offered foods. At the same time, a line on the right-hand bottom corner of the screen says, "Results not typical."

I wondered what result was not typical. Was it that people who use this product end up on TV promoting it? Or that people who use the product actually lose weight? Or that people who eat the advertised food actually think it is any good? Maybe "Results not typical" refers to all three. One has to wonder given the schlock nature of the ad just what warning their fine print is conveying.

Of course, sadly, the ad would not be running, and it has been around awhile, if it did not work in attracting people to use the product. We should all be aware of the weakness of the case study approach and approaches that claim success without appropriate experimental design. How would you evaluate the above statement if you treated her claim, "eat this food and lose weight" as an organizational program or initiative and wanted to determine if in fact you could place any stock in those claims?

Program evaluation suffers a history of skepticism often due a history of poorly conceived evaluation methodologies. One of the most widely used designs for program evaluation is one in which 1) a single group is given a baseline measure, then 2) the program is implemented and then 3) a post implementation measurement is made to determine the effect of the program. This approach is fraught with problems. Let me illustrate. Let's use the following statement as an example:

A school system wants to know if the investment it is making in advanced teacher training is improving educational attainment among its students.

In this example, a baseline measure regarding standardized student achievement test scores is collected prior to the implementation of the new teacher-training program. In addition, surveys can be done of the students asking about their comfort and mastery with the subjects covered by the teacher-training program. After the teachers receive their training and the next class of students comes through, the measurement process is repeated. Students on average now report that they feel more comfortable with the targeted subjects and test scores are moving up. The teacher-training program is determined to be a success and additional funds are poured into teacher training. What was not taken into consideration using this approach is the fact that the students got new textbooks with vastly improved course material and the class schedule was redesigned so that the students spent more time on the targeted subjects. What was thought to be an outcome of teacher training was actually better course material and more time spent devoted to the subject.

Various approaches could improve the ability of the school system to improve its evaluation. Here is one. If the above field experiment had been carried out as follows, the results would have been much clearer. In this alternative approach, the same setup is used, but only half the teachers in the first round receive the training. When the next round of students come through the program, the students whose teachers received the training are compared to those whose teachers did not (a control group), holding everything else constant. Holding everything else constant in this case means that all students received the new texts and all students had their schedules changed. Now when we compare the students whose teachers received the training to those who did not, we might find that all student scores improved, but the students whose teachers received the advanced training had even higher scores and felt even more comfortable regarding their mastery of the subject than those students whose teachers did not. In this case, a more confident determination can be made that the advanced teacher training did help to improve test scores.

The criticism of this approach is that it is not right to withhold a potentially beneficial experience from those in the control group. And the answer to that is, in certain circumstances, it is not right to withhold that potential benefit (experimental drugs being used in life threatening circumstances is one case). However, in the above example, it is truly unclear whether there is any benefit to the students whose teachers went through the advanced training versus those who did not. And there certainly would be a long-term benefit to the school system by knowing the true impact of that training experience.

ABNORMAL CHANGE

SATURDAY, APRIL 5, 2008

PERFORMANCE

The other day, a friend asked me, "How far back can you remember?" I thought about it for a while searching my old memories and finally responded "Maybe 28 or 30." "Years ago?" he asked. "No, waist size," I responded. Change happens.

Dandelions are the perennial weed that are just about impossible to get rid of. Tough as nails, they show up everywhere you don't want them to. Upon closer inspection, the yellow flower is actually made up of numerous small flowers, each yellow petal being a separate flower capable of turning into an individual seed and in aggregate yielding the cottony ball that was so much fun to blow upon and scatter so long ago. I can remember that. Dandelions are adaptable. One study of them recently showed that in as little as 12 generations dandelions adapted from having that familiar cottony seed distribution system, with seeds drifting in the wind, to one that favored seeds that fell immediately around the mother (and father since they are asexual) plant. The plant was able to evolve, incorporating a new adaptation in as little as 12 seasons. The new adaptation was the development of seeds without the white cottony tufts upon which to float in the wind.

What was the reason for this change? When dandelions found themselves growing in urban locations with concrete all around, it became more advantageous to them to fall immediately next to mom, who was already conveniently gowning in a crack in the sidewalk filled with soil, then to scatter seeds in all directions looking for the next bit of dirt in which to put down roots. In as little as 12 seasons, dandelions took an evolutionary process that is often viewed as glacially slow and made dramatic change.

Organizations, of course, need to be able to change or they will eventually die out, advice that any dandelion can give. A critically important point about organizational change though is that the most successful organizations need to consider how to control the definition of what are the normal standards of performance for their products and services. Being able to control the definition of standard or normal can be a path to greatly increasing market share and profitability. This is as true for the little restaurant on the corner as it is for the global behemoth. Organizations that can control the definition of "normal" performance or "normal" service are the standard-bearers in their respective markets. Being able to control the definition of normal is also how some upstart startup can shake up an industry and penetrate the traditional barriers to competition.

Federal Express changed the definition of "normal" delivery times for packages and letters, doing something that no one else seemed to consider and grew into an extremely profitable, very successful organization. The company again changed the definition of what a customer could expect when tracking packages, greatly increasing transparency and again setting the standard that everyone strove to emulate.

Henry Ford, with his concept of mass production, changed the definition of what a "normal" car should cost, greatly increasing the ability for the average person to own a personal transportation machine. His working definition of affordability was that a Ford Motor Company worker on the assembly line should be able to afford the product that they were producing.

The Japanese car companies, Toyota, Honda, Nissan among others, came along much later and changed the definition of what normal quality was, tapping into a desire of the consumer to own a quality, gas efficient, reliable product with fewer defects at a reasonable cost and quickly captured enormous market share. (They did not start out that way, but came to see the light as they evolved and adopted the six-sigma tools made available by Dr. Deming).

Apple, a company that takes the notion of owning the "norm" seriously, changed the definition of how we buy and purchase music, driving traditional retail record stores to near or into bankruptcy, as they could not adapt their traditional retail model. Apple is trying to do that again with the iPhone.

Amazon changed the way we purchase products online and Google changed the norm by which we search for and access information. eBay forever changed the way that garage or lawn sales happen and has spurred an entire secondary economy employing hundreds of thousands.

Starbucks changed the definition of how you purchase coffee and how much it costs. For a long time now, a cup of high-octane coffee has cost more than a gallon of high-octane gasoline, but I think gasoline is pulling ahead once again. I cannot help but wonder if part of what is happening with the new highs in gasoline prices is to establish a new norm around what a gallon of gas should cost. (I can remember the 60s—cents per gallon).

Wal-Mart established a new norm around pricing models and Target and Kohl's added in more of a quality and shopping experience component (where did I hear that before?). A similar battle rages between Home Depot and Lowe's. The list goes on and on.

The challenge to organizations as they seek to improve their performance is not to simply incrementally improve. It is to strive for breakthroughs that allow them to leapfrog the competition—to create not simply normal change, but abnormal change, change beyond what is expected; to reinvent not only themselves but their products in such a fashion that it creates a new standard, a new norm of performance and then to make it happen. This takes creativity and insight. It takes a workforce that is willing and ready to adapt to new ideas and concepts and can work outside the box. To paraphrase one company's motto, "We have a better idea"—do you?

Heart of Hearts

Friday, April 18, 2008

Talent

There is an old story that describes a very special clock. This clock does not work like most clocks, keeping track of the passage of time. Rather this clock, though it looks like a regular clock, keeps track of the time until a certain event is supposed to happen. It counts down the days, hours and minutes until that moment occurs. What strikes me about this is not that you can create a clock that is a countdown timer, but that a single aspect of reality can be thought of in distinctly two fashions. One is to keep track of the passage of time and the other is to keep track of time until an event is to occur, one aspect of reality, time and two distinct points of view about how to measure it. The clocks can look identical, both are measuring time, yet they operate in distinctly differing fashions.

As I spend more and more time with various organizations, I am struck by another duality of what I view as another single aspect of reality. And that reality is how employees are viewed. In order to make the point, I will put it into stark terms using extreme descriptions while realizing that most organizations do not fall at one extreme or the other.

At one extreme, there are management teams of organizations that truly believe that their success is because of their employees and at the other extreme, you have management teams that view employees as costs to be controlled, two extreme points on one scale. And to me there is a very interesting part to this concept. On the surface, it can be extremely difficult to tell the difference between these two groups. Much of what they do looks similar. Among the one group's goals will be to retain the valuable assets called employees. Among the other group's goals will be to make sure everyone is replaceable—that the cogs in the wheel are easily replaced should one fall off.

Both groups will have impressive plaques on the wall describing their mission, vision and values. Both groups will say things like, "employees are our most important asset." Both could have certain employee benefit programs. And both could be very respectful of employees, treating them well and providing opportunity for all to succeed—in good times. The difference is more obvious when there is an economic downturn, or when an organization feels stress.

In the organizations that view employees as the true reason for their success, an overriding theme seems to permeate. What can we do to help make our employees more capable of success? How can we knock down the barriers that get in their way, those things that prevent them from performing? How can we enable them more? How do we maintain the motivation that they brought with them when they first came to this job?

It has been documented repeatedly that the most positive employees in most organizations are the ones you just hired and it takes the average organization about three years to beat that "positiveness" out of them. What happens to the employees that their degree of positiveness flags? The data suggest that they begin dealing more and more with the organization's bureaucracy. They are not given the same amount of attention as when they first joined up. Their jobs did not deliver on the salary expectations they may have thought were there. They were not given recognition for their performance over time. They did not advance as quickly as they thought and in fact, they seem to feel that their talents are not being recognized. Realistic job previews help in this area, but they are only part of the answer and this pattern of decline is not necessarily seen in all organizations, but is seen in a relatively large number of them.

Some management teams upon hearing this will think to themselves, "Well then, turnover is not so bad. After all, as we hire new people, we will get people with more positive attitudes and hey, if they stick around for three years or so, great. We can just hire more replacements at that time." People after all are just costs to be controlled.

Other management teams will view the turnover as a loss of organizational memory, and with that, goes capability and long-standing relationships with others that can characterize successful organizations. While some of this comes from Wall Street and its resultant short-term orientation, with managers of today feeling intense pressure to make their profit numbers, I think another component of this comes from the heart. I think some managers in their heart-of-hearts believe that the path to organizational success is through their employees and others believe that employees are simply part of the problem, preventing organizations from being as profitable as they could be. I think it shows up in hundreds of subtle ways and some not so subtle ways in the day-to-day actions of the organization.

In some recent conversations I have had with senior managers of various types on this idea, I get general agreement, but I also get a good deal of discomfort. It seems that some organizational managers do not necessarily want to operate in this fashion, but feel that because everyone else is, in order to remain competitive they have to as well. What may cause this to show up more starkly once again is that we are now in a period of economic uncertainty, with many betting that we are already in a recession and speculating on how long it will last. Some organizations will immediately go to layoffs, cutting off those expenses called employees, while others will try to figure out how to better utilize those assets called employees to help weather the storm.

Wayne Cascio, a professor of management and international business at the University of Colorado in Denver has conducted a series of studies and has published a book on alternatives to layoffs in down cycles. He has found that those companies that follow these practices of retaining valuable employees, treating them as assets, in the long-term, outperform those that quickly resort to layoffs. He finds that those companies that "view their workers as assets to be developed rather than costs to be cut" will be more likely to succeed. "In general, we found that it was just not possible for firms to 'save' or 'shrink' their way to prosperity."

But in order to operate in this fashion, the organization has to believe, it has to believe in its employees in its heart of hearts.

Fears of Birds

Saturday, April 26, 2008

Talent

Can a bird be afraid of heights? Can a fish fear water? Do earthworms worry about germs that might exist in the soil? Can a raccoon fear the dark? Animals, when in their natural habitats, are unlikely to show fear for things that are part of their very existence. However, fear can be learned and once learned, can be debilitating.

There is an old children's story of a fish that angered the village elders by slapping an elder with his tail. The elders were then caught up in debate, trying to decide on a suitable punishment for the disrespectful fish. They thought about eating him, but decided that since captured fish are eaten anyway, that wouldn't be a punishment. They thought about hanging him, but realized that the fish had no neck. After much deliberation, during which time the fish was carefully taken care of, since the punishment would not be as meaningful if the fish was sick or injured, they decided to drown the fish. They took the fish, which was swimming vigorously and had gained quite a bit of weight while in the care of the elders, to a nearby lake and threw him in. Since the fish was never seen or caught again, they assumed their punishment had worked and that the fish had drowned.

When employees come to work for a new organization, are promoted or assume new responsibilities, they most typically display a great deal of excitement about the new job or opportunity. They are in their element and know no fear. Most people, when given a chance to achieve and are appropriately rewarded for their accomplishments, revel in the opportunity made available. The data demonstrating this is unequivocal. It is typically only after time, during which they are interacting with the organization and the environment that the excitement often diminishes. The challenge to the organization and those living within it is how to make it a part of the typical employee's very existence? How do you make the organization part of the employee's natural element? How do you make an employee take to an organization as a fish would take to water?

Not everyone is a perfect fit for every organization, but since we also know that in general, people are looking for the same fundamentals out of the work environment regardless of generation, gender, geography or ethnicity, most people (assuming they came in with the appropriate skill set) have what it takes to succeed in most organizations. The organization's environment is typically the reason for failure.

Humans are not natural creatures of the air, of the night, the earth, oceans or space. We don't fly on our evolutionarily provided wings, soaring through the clouds or use our gills to swim in the ocean's depths. We are a social species and are natural creatures of our brains. We use our brains to dream of soaring and then we fashion wings upon which we can soar. And those of us who dreamed of soaring revel in the act of flying upon the realization of our dreams. Our birds show no fear of flying. When sufficiently motivated, when appropriately organized, we realize our dreams.

Sweet Dreams

Tuesday, March 25, 2008

Off the Cuff

I want to build a shining city on a hill. Day-to-day, sometimes you wonder what all the activity we engage in means. Why are we here? What are we supposed to be accomplishing? Any rational-thinking human will have thoughts like these at some point.

I had a professor who told me that neurotics build castles in the sky and psychotics live in them. Well, I don't think I am neurotic or psychotic, but I want to build, to create, a shining city on a hill. What do I mean? I would like to be part of creating an environment where people are excited about being part of something truly special. A place where each member has opportunities to excel and to develop to their fullest potential. A place where they cannot only fully contribute organizationally, they are not simply rewarded for their efforts, but *feel* rewarded by their efforts. A place where people feel like their efforts have an impact on broadly benefiting humanity. I want to build an organization where people can be intellectually stimulated to question and probe why things are done the way they are in the spirit of continual improvement, not only for the organization, but also for those served by the organization. I want them, and I guess by extension, myself, to feel like what we are doing really matters in the greater scheme of things. I want people to laugh, to have joy with and in their work. Is this a general path to fulfillment or simply my own path?

We were traveling out of town for a family event. When we got to the hotel, I was pretty exhausted by the long drive. We had dinner with some relatives and after that, I was ready to put my head on the pillow and get some shuteye. Our room had a king sized bed. So, my wife and I, along with my eight year old, decided to just share one bed rather than opening the couch. We all fell asleep rather quickly and after a few hours, I was awakened by my daughter laughing in her sleep. I lay there listening to her laughter and realized that I would be very content to listen to her laugh and her sweet dreams all night long. I was sure I would be up in the morning feeling refreshed from that experience. Even now as I think of it, it brings a smile to my face.

Building an organization where people can laugh, where there is a joy to their work may be an overlooked critical aspect of organizational development. There are, however, some advocates of laughter at work. For instance, the Global Coaches Network on its website claims that:

- Laughter increases productivity
- Those who laugh out loud are more creative at problem solving than those who don't
- Those who laugh have better memory retention than those who don't
- Those who laugh have less stress and miss less time from work than those who don't
- Laughter is a major coping mechanism
- Those who laugh together may work more effectively together than those who don't

I don't know if these statements are backed up by research, but they certainly feel right. It reminds me of the old vaudeville joke.

A man walks into the doctor's office saying, "doctor, doctor it hurts when I do this," (picture man bending his arm) and of course, the doctor's response is "don't do that."

Well, when we laugh at work, we are running into the doctor's office saying "doctor, doctor I feel better when I laugh" and the response from the doctor (in this case, I like to picture the doctor as an Industrial/Organizational Psychologist) is "you should laugh more."

I can't imagine that I am alone in wishing for this sweet dream and I hope there are many of you who are interested in laughing more and finding joy in and at our work.

40:1

MONDAY, MARCH 31, 2008

PERFORMANCE

Spring is once again struggling to exert its dominance over the winter months, while signs of the coming thaw are emerging. Recently, I spotted a pair of hooded mergansers, three pairs of wood ducks, several mallards and one pair of geese on my pond. Robins have been jumping up and down on the lawn conducting their traditional mating dance, and daffodils are doing their best to poke their leaves above the ground—all harbingers of the coming season.

In another annual rite of spring, we traveled to Vermont over a weekend, a nearly four hour trek, to the annual Maple Syrup festival. We went sugaring, visiting four farms that produce maple syrup. At one farm, there were approximately 50 – 75 new born baby lambs and some new born baby pigs. Interestingly, sheep usually have one lamb born at a time, a ratio of one offspring for each ewe, or 1:1. But they may have up to three, a ratio of 3:1. Pigs, of course, are in a whole different category with large numbers born per sow. The new mother we saw had nine piglets suckling, a ratio of 9:1. However, it was difficult to determine an exact count with all the little piglet bodies pushed up against the mother.

1, 1, 2, 3, 5, 8, 13, 21 is part of a famous sequence of numbers made even more famous by the book and movie "The Da Vinci Code." Called the Fibonacci sequence, each number in the string is the sum of the previous two, a simple rule. The sequence, along with other related mathematical sequences, show up in places that some people would consider unexpected. In nature, as you look at objects as diverse as pine cones, leaf growth and galaxies, this sequence, or closely related sequences of numbers, comes into play. The sequence of numbers represents the outcome when certain simple rules of nature are followed. For the buds on a cone of a spruce tree, the rule, which is chemically driven, seems to form a new bud that will turn into a needle—as distantly as possible from the last bud that formed on the cone. As this rule is followed, a spiral pattern of new needles forms, which follows the golden ratio, or the Fibonacci sequence. If you have every closely examined the cone of a spruce tree you realize that from these simple rules, tremendous complexity can emerge.

Complex flight patterns and flocking behavior of birds were simulated by Craig Reynolds in a program called "Boids." He showed that three rules can be used to describe the behaviors of flocks of birds. He called the rules *Separation, Alignment* and *Cohesion*. The *Separation* rule was for steering to avoid crowding local flock mates—don't hit anyone. The *Alignment* rule was for steering to the average heading of the local flock—go in the direction that most everyone else is. The *Cohesion* rule was for steering to the average position of the others in the local flock—don't lose sight of your friends. Applying these three simple rules allowed Reynolds to create a *simulation of complex bird flocking* patterns.

In the maple sugaring process, tree sap is gathered from sugar maples, traditionally in galvanized steel buckets hanging from taps driven into the trees. In larger operations, the sap is collected by a series of plastic tubes leading from the tree downhill to a collection point. One farm that we visited had tapped 7,000 trees, another had tapped 9,000. Sap starts to run when you have cold nights, 20 degrees Fahrenheit or lower, warmer days, 40 degrees and above. A fifth generation farmer told me that it looked like it was going to be a very good harvest this year. So far, nearly two-thirds of the way into the season, he had already produced 2,000 gallons of maple syrup, where most years in total he would produce between 1,400 and 1,600 gallons (a gallon of freshly made maple syrup sells for between $36 and $40 dollars at the farm).

In order to produce 2,000 gallons of syrup, 80,000 gallons of maple sap must be boiled down, a ratio of 40:1. That is a lot of sap, a lot of raw product that is needed to produce one gallon of fine Vermont maple syrup. It is as though you are concentrating the essence of the tree as you create maple syrup. Collected sap, fresh from the trees, sits inside a large tank, external to the sugar house. A pipe from that tank leads into an evaporator in the sugar house. (Prior to the sap going into the evaporator, some water is removed using a reverse osmosis process.)

In the evaporator, there is a channel, a pathway through the evaporator that the sap follows. It enters in one end as a cold raw ingredient. As it travels to the other end, it boils away the water leaving the maple syrup concentrate. Once the sap boils at 219 degrees (this temperature is adjusted based on altitude), or seven degrees above the boiling point of water, you have maple syrup. This syrup drains out of the evaporator, and is then filtered, graded by color and bottled. From a large amount of raw ingredients, a gem of a final product emerges. However, you must follow a simple rule: the syrup is not ready unless it boils at 219 degrees. If it boils at a lower temperature, it is not sufficiently concentrated. If it boils at a higher temperature, it will result in maple candy, not syrup.

New research on insights, solutions to problems or paths forward for solving issues has been emerging recently. Some findings indicate that along with unique patterns of electrical activity in the brain, prior to moments of insight, there is a simple rule that if followed, can lead to moments of inspiration. This simple rule is to expand the number of possible solutions, to broaden one's horizon, allowing new combinations of solutions to emerge for potential consideration. As new interconnections between possibilities are generated, a potential solution, leading to a breakthrough or sudden insight can emerge—a so-called "A-ha!" moment. A 2004 research study documented that just prior to reporting a sudden insight, subjects had a large amount of electrical activity in the right brain region responsible for integrating pieces of information, however distant.

It is as though you are starting with a large amount of raw ingredients, potential solutions, and running these ideas through an evaporator, your brain. When an idea reaches the right temperature, out pops your final product—a potentially novel solution that can hopefully be implemented successfully. The ratio of sap to syrup, of raw ingredients to final product, 40:1, might not be too far off from what you should aim for as you consider potential solutions to your more vexing problems.

Bay-of-Pigs thinking, or *Groupthink,* is when members of a group try to minimize potential conflict in the group and reach consensus without critically testing and analyzing alternative ideas. It is as though one idea floats to the top, possibly promulgated by a leader within the group, and without group members feeling that alternatives can be raised, it is explored for possible implementation. The reasons that this type of thinking occurs vary. However, some potential reasons why group members may avoid raising alternatives is to avoid looking foolish, assuming that others know more than they do, to avoid conflict with other group members or to prevent isolationism from others within the group—a punishment for not falling into line. For those presenting ideas that become part of the *Groupthink* process, it can be a matter of control over the group, a matter of power display.

Avoiding *Groupthink* and finding moments of insight and novel solutions might be as easy as remembering a simple, easy to follow ratio. *40:1*—from simple rules, sometimes tremendously great ideas can emerge.

WHAT MAKES A GOOD EMPLOYEE SURVEY QUESTION–101

TUESDAY, DECEMBER 25, 2007

EMPLOYEE RESEARCH

I was asked to put together suggestions for good employee survey questions to illustrate poorly written items and to make suggestions on how they could be improved. Here is what I have come up with.* Qualities of good employee engagement survey questions mean that:

1) *They are actionable.* The results I receive direct me to do something rather than leave me wondering what the answers really mean.

2) *They are specific.* The questions deal with one concept at a time so separate issues are not confused with one another.

3) *They are simple.* There are no words or concepts that could be interpreted three different ways by three different people.

4) *They have been proven effective.* The questions deal with issues that have been found historically to matter or are considered important to the business (as opposed to issues like the quality of the cafeteria food).

Here are examples of employee survey questions, or items, which have been used previously, but will likely not provide what you hope or need. I have also given revised statements for how the items could be improved.

Ineffective: "What ____% of people need our protective products?"
Scale choices: 81% or more; 80 – 61%; 60 – 41%; 40 – 21%; 20% or less

> **The problem:** Among the issues with this item is a scale that assumes a level of precision that is impossible for respondents to give.

> **Better:** Overall, rate our ability as a company in turning potential customers (people who are considering our protective products) into purchasers of our products."
> Scale choices: Very Good; Good; Average; Poor; Very Poor

Ineffective: "If I should find myself in a jam at work, I could get out of it because I've experienced jams before."

> **The problem:** This is attempting to measure personal characteristics of the worker—the ability to get out of a jam—because of experience. How would the organization improve on this if the results came back poorly? Give people more experience with jams? Organizational surveys should focus on organizational characteristics that the organization can actually improve upon. The uncommonly used word "jam" is also likely to be misunderstood (especially internationally), creating varying interpretations.

> **Better:** "In general, when problems arise at work, I have the resources I need at my disposal to resolve them."

Ineffective: "I do good work."

>**The problem:** Come on—it is virtually impossible for someone in a normal state of mind to rate his or her own work negatively.

>**Better:** "The quality of products and services that this organization delivers are among the best in our industry."

Ineffective: "In your opinion, how limiting are the following obstacles to your career advancement at [company x]?"

>"a. Stereotypes about my commitment or abilities based on my gender"

>**The problem:** The question presumes the company has this obstacle rather than using wording to cull out potential problems that are actionable.

>**Better:** "Advancement here is based on merit. The most deserving, regardless of their background or 'who they know,' get ahead."

Ineffective: "It is easy for me to complete work assignments and projects within this company."

>**The problem:** This item comes with a built-in bias—easy is good. It may be that the difficult assignments get employees' juices flowing. It is more important to know whether workers are given what they need to accomplish their assignments, regardless of whether projects are easy or difficult.

>**Better:** "I am provided with the tools and resources I need to accomplish my work."

Ineffective: "My benefits are better here than the benefits at other companies."

> **The problem:** This question is setting up the organization for failure. It is extremely rare for a company today to have a goal of "unsurpassed benefits."
>
> **Better:** "The benefits I receive are fair." Or "My benefits are comparable to the benefits I would receive elsewhere."

Ineffective: "Employees are encouraged to work as a team."

> **The problem:** The underlying issue here is aspiration versus actuality. The question doesn't go far enough—is teamwork actually happening? An organization may say it encourages teamwork, but if its rewards system actually discourages it, teamwork won't happen.
>
> **Better:** "Where I work, we act as a team to accomplish our tasks."

Ineffective: "The organizational structure here is meaningful to me."

> **The problem:** "Meaningful" in this context is a vague word that will be interpreted by each employee in his or her own way.
>
> **Better:** "Our organizational structure is enabling in that it helps us get our work done effectively."

Ineffective: "The business policies, standards of performance and conduct here are seriously emphasized throughout the whole company."

The problem: Too many questions are being asked at the same time, so any answer will be hard to interpret. The question also assumes employees know what is happening elsewhere, which is never a good assumption.

Better: "Where I work, the organizational standards of conduct are emphasized."

My co-workers Sara Weiner, Ph.D., Jeffrey Jolton, Ph.D. Scott Brooks, Ph.D. and Bryan Hayes, Ph.D. all helped me out by submitting ideas for this piece.

Employee Survey Interpretation–101

101

Friday, February 1, 2008

Employee Research

An executive of a financial institution was examining his employee survey results. He was very pleased with the findings and was especially pleased with the comparisons of his institution to the outside world on common items, or norms. On each item that we went over, his smile grew larger and larger as he saw that his institution was among the top performing organizations—until we got to pay. When people in his organization were asked to rate their pay, they responded in a typical or about average fashion. He asked, "How can I be such a top performer in so many areas and be merely average on how people rate their pay?" I asked him what pay strategy his organization used, and without skipping a beat he replied, "To pay about average." He was expecting halo—that exceptional responses to one area of the survey would bleed over to other areas and give average findings a boost. I indicated that people actually read the items and differentiate among them, scoring average on average performing items and above average on strengths of the organization.

When we receive survey responses, we can often struggle to interpret the meaning behind the numbers. While not everyone needs to use a similar approach to gain insight into the employee survey data, in the following sections, I outline of an approach that I use to obtain a preliminary view of an organization's employee survey findings—an assessment of its culture.

The first thing I like to do is to look at the results in an absolute fashion, simply meaning, what is the percent favorable, neutral and unfavorable? I like to start down at the item level to get a better sense of what is happening in the organization, looking at the details, and then working my way up to any dimensions or indices that are included in the survey. One common misperception about survey findings is that the results are a like a school's report card, where traditionally a score of 90% or better is an "A," 80% is a "B" and 70% a "C." This is not an accurate analogy—a better one is to say that survey results are more like election results, if you get more than 50%, you win (in a two party election).

I first look at the favorable side of the item responses (typically top 2-box on a five-point scale). I would call 50 – 65% "moderately favorable;" 65 – 75% "favorable" and more than 75% positive, "strongly favorable." I then turn to the other end of the spectrum and look at the responses in the bottom 2-boxes. I become concerned when about one out of five, or 20%, of people are negative. As the negativity grows to about one out of three, or 33%, my concern increasingly grows; when it hits two out of five, or 40%, the organization needs to very clearly understand the issues that the item response represents.

I find it very helpful to picture the responses in terms of headcount—for instance, one out of two people feel this way—and then ask myself, is this acceptable? What does this mean in terms of organizational performance? What I literally do as a first pass is take a sheet of paper and draw a line down the middle. On one side, I start listing out the items that are at 75% or more favorable and on the other side, I start listing out those that are 25% or more negative. The cut scores are not necessarily cast in concrete, and I will modify them if the data for the organization is exceptionally high or low.

I also examine the total pattern of responses across all of the response choices and take special note of where the middle "neutral" choice is larger than about 25%. I will also keep a look out for a few other patterns. For instance, if you have a roughly equal distribution across the favorable, neutral and unfavorable choices, it is called a "mixed" response. If you ask three people their opinion on this topic, you receive three different answers. This could be indicative of a lack of clarity or a very uneven performance on the item.

Large neutrals are valid and they usually do not mean that someone has no opinion; they mean that someone has an opinion and the opinion is neutral. For instance, if you ask a room full of people to rate the taste of vanilla ice cream on a scale of one to three—to keep it simple—where a one is "I love it, it is my favorite flavor;" a three is "I dislike it, I will do anything to avoid eating it;" and a two is "not my favorite, but if it is in front of me it will disappear," the vast majority of people choose two. Does this mean they have no opinion on the taste of vanilla ice cream? Of course not. They have an opinion and the opinion is "middle of the road," not strongly positive or negative. It is valid, it is real and it is not negative or positive.

Once I have my two lists, I take a step back and try to see how the items listed hang together, if at all. For instance, is the positive side of the page dominated by items dealing with treatment or customer focus? Does the negative side deal with items surrounding employees' career opportunities?

Once this is done, I do a second pass through the items. This time, I am doing a comparative analysis. I will compare the responses from each item to the larger group of which the organization is part—so a department within a plant will be contrasted against the results for the entire plant. I will also contrast the findings against external norms and internal benchmarks. Often these surveys are census surveys with very large numbers involved, so statistical relevance is really not meaningful when trying to decide if a group is similar, more or less favorable than the comparison group.

If you go back into organizations after surveys are run over time, interview people in those organizations and ask them when the place began "feeling" any different to them, the following pattern tends to emerge. At about a five point difference (more or less favorable), people begin to say things like "I can't quite put my finger on it, but we may be improving," (or declining as the case may be). Five points seems to be a "just noticeable difference." At 10 points, people say things like "things are moving in the right (or wrong) direction. And at 15 points, people use words like "feels completely different." So again, I take out my paper and draw a line down the middle. On one side, I list out where the organization is 10 points or more higher than the comparison and on the other side, where the organization is 10 points or more lower. (I realize that you can use excel for these exercises, but my old habits die hard).

So now I have a list of key strengths (more than 75% favorable), key issues (more than 25% negative), and the places in which the organization is more favorable and less favorable than the comparison groups in a meaningful way. I repeat these steps at the dimension level. I next put the findings through my exception filters.

One finding that is very common is that more senior people in the hierarchy tend to be more favorable in their survey responses than less senior ones. While not every survey asks for this demographic, those surveys that do and then looking for exceptions to this finding can add insight. There are some exceptions to this pattern. When asking about quality or customer service, it is not unusual to find the more senior folks to be more critical.

So I now look at the responses surrounding strategy, communications and decision making, etc. I look to see if the expected pattern holds. And where it doesn't hold—say for instance if middle managers look more like hourly workers on understanding strategy—I make note of it. What I am looking for here are exceptions to typically seen patterns because these exceptions add insight into what is going on within the organization.

Another exception filter that I use is reserved for "zero tolerance items." These are health and safety items, harassment or discrimination items, ethics items, etc. In essence, these are items where anything less than 100% favorable is not acceptable. I throw out the guidelines that I listed above and list out any items that need to score 100%.

A third filter I use deals with strategy, but in many cases, it is only possible for someone internal to the client company to use this filter. Surveys can tell you the state of the environment, at this moment in time, within the organization. What they cannot tell you is that with the pressures and challenges facing the organization over the next five years, *this* is the focus of where the company should go strategically. The survey is a good jumping off point, but one role of management is to strategically decide that to compete successfully in their market niche, with their products, *this* is where the organization should be on certain items. For example, the leadership may decide to work on innovation, customer focus or on responsiveness. An interpretation of the results can benefit by taking this into consideration.

A closely related filter has to do with what the organization needs to be "the best in the world" at. I would argue that no organization had the ability, the resources, the time and the funds to be the best in the world at everything. And in fact, if you pair up two of the items on the survey, you may find them to be somewhat contradictory and it may be impossible to excel at both. For instance, if you are the most innovative or most responsive, it is difficult or impossible to be the best value. In order to be the best value, cost cutting tends to obstruct being the most innovative or responsive. So a strategic decision that leadership must make is to determine what it will do exceptionally well. What will it be the best in the world at and what will it accept being average at?

I will then examine the items through another template, which I call Message, Performance and Future. These are defined below:

Message: These are items that have to do with how the organization describes itself to employees and identifies its role in it. These items deal with clarity regarding what the organization is about, how it will operate and how each person contributes in delivering on those goals. Is there an inspiring mission? Importantly, are the organizational communications delivering that Message consistent throughout all levels of the organization? Are policies and practices in line with that Message? Is it clear what each person's role is in support of the Message?

Performance: These are items that deal with people getting what they need to be able to deliver on the Message—to get the job done. Performance should be thought of in the broadest sense, including teamwork, effective management, communications, decision making, training, equipment, resources, processes and procedures.

Future: These are items that give people a sense of a longer-term benefit to being associated with the organization, including having a positive future and a sense of belonging, of being valued by the organization. These are the compelling reasons for them to stick around for the long-term with the organization.

The items that I have now placed onto my various lists can fall (sometimes with a bit of gray) into one of these categories. It can be very helpful for an organization to see that its issues are all about Message or are restricted to Performance. It can help point them in the right direction from an action standpoint.

While no two organizations are absolutely identical, no two analyses need be either. However, a consistent approach to an analysis, even if it just personal preference, can make the interpretation of your findings a bit easier.

Employee Survey Interpretation-102

102

Thursday, February 7, 2008

Employee Research

*"If you were really good, you could get all you needed simply
by asking one question."*
—Anonymous manager discussing his survey results

Over the last decade or so, there has been increasing pressure on
survey providers to make their employee surveys shorter and more
of the items directly actionable. People in general can answer four
to five questions per minute and so the difference between a long
survey, say 100 items, and a shorter one, say 50 items, is about 10
minutes. Concerns on survey length seem to center on perceptions
of the burden placed on the individual and the organization rather
then the actual amount of time spent answering questions.

Let me state something fairly obvious: surveys can only provide
feedback on what was asked about. If you don't ask a survey
participant, "Do you have the training you need to get your job
done," you can't expect to answer the question from the survey itself,
"Do people have the training they need?"

Survey questions can be thought of as falling broadly into two
categories (plus demographics). One category is called dependent
variables and the other is called independent variables. Dependent
variables are outcome items (e.g. overall satisfaction, pride,

intention to leave) and independent variables are causative or action oriented items. In experiments, independent variables are the factors that a researcher can manipulate to try and tease out cause and effect on the studied outcome or dependent variable. For instance, if I give more training, does pride go up? Does intention to leave decline?

While a good survey can benefit from a mix of both, one of the consequences of shorter surveys is more of a reliance on dependent items, which can be more broad and general. In some cases, independent variables can become or can be treated as dependent variables, and to a lesser extent, dependent variables can become independent ones.

In surveys, one easy way to tell if a question is dependent or independent is to determine if impacting the item's result directly is possible. If, for instance, you ask someone to rate his/her pride in working for the organization and the result comes back poorly, the next step is to think about raising the level of pride in the organization. In order to do that, you need to consider the factors within the organization that impact pride. Your ability to impact the level of pride in the organization is determined by your ability to impact those factors that you hypothesize drive pride. Hence, the question about pride is a dependent variable and not directly actionable.

If the result from the item "Do you have the training you need to get your job done?" was poor, in order to improve on the item, you would provide training, hopefully the kind of training people need to accomplish their jobs. Since the result from this item is directly actionable, it is an independent variable.

You can see that if you were to ask about each and every potential specific action that enables job performance, you would wind up with a very lengthy questionnaire. You would ask about the training (for your current job to prepare you for the next job), communications (upwards, downwards, lateral, timeliness, openness, honesty of), decision making (speed and quality), cooperation and teamwork, information systems, equipment and resources, computer systems hardware and software, accuracy of company data, inventory systems, maintenance and repairs, physical working conditions, safety, ethics, clarity of company mission, vision and values, etc. the list could go on and on. And that is the rub. The push to shorten questionnaires leads to a greater reliance on dependent variables and results in fewer directly actionable items being used—in direct opposition to the pressures that organizations are putting on survey providers.

To shorten the above list, you might ask "Do you have what you need to get your job done?" instead of each and every specific aspect of the job. While the result of that item is important, it is not directly actionable without asking people in follow-up meetings "What do you need in order to get your job done better?" (That is the real power behind survey feedback meetings—to put specifics onto the actions that should be taken).

One approach that can be taken in analyzing survey results is to take one of the dependent variables and regress it against the independent variables (through correlations, regression or modeling techniques)—for instance, taking pride as the dependent variable or outcome item, and then statistically determining which other items from the survey (it is best to limit it to the other independent or actionable survey items) are most influential on causing pride to go up becoming more favorable or to decline becoming less favorable. These lists of "key drivers" can help answer the questions about how to create positive change in the dependent variable results. It does not negate the underlying truth, however, that the survey can only provide results on items that you ask about. There may be other drivers of pride within the organization that are not asked about on the survey and hence, cannot possibly show up on the key driver list.

Employee Survey Interpretation-103

103

Saturday, February 16, 2008

Employee Research

One way to help prioritize the findings from an employee survey that an organization should focus on has to do with the items from the survey that are found to "link" most strongly to various business or organizational performance metrics. These linkages can offer guidance on where resources should be spent to have the largest potential payback to the organization.

We perform linkages in our mind on a routine basis to help us prioritize all of our activities and to help us direct our energy. Hypothesized linkages are rigorously debated publicly as policy matters. For instance, one debated linkage is between the playing of violent video games and increased violence in the behavior of children. What about the effect of watching violent cartoons or movies? Will the increase in troop strength in Iraq, the "surge," help to stabilize the situation? One group hypothesizing a linkage feels it will; another group says it will have no or little effect. Even after it has occurred, the hypothesized linkage is not always clear as many other factors, other than the surge itself, come into play. Will the tax rebate that is being prepared for distribution this May actually spur the economy? Is there a link? If the money had been used in another fashion, would the positive effect on the economy be greater? Because of the large number of moving pieces, the number of variables to be taken into account when answering this question means that the ultimate answer is unlikely to be exceedingly clear.

This same kind of linkage logic in a simplified fashion can be used in helping to determine the employee survey items that should be acted upon, hopefully with more clarity. Will improving on the speed of decision making have a greater impact on organizational performance than providing additional training for staff on how to perform their jobs? What if decision making was moderately favorably rated, but training was poorly rated? Which action would have a greater impact in this situation? What if the ratings were reversed? It can become rather complicated, but it doesn't need to be.

Linkages can be done at a single point in time (a concurrent study) or they can be done over a period of time (a predictive study). A third approach is a bit forensic in nature—looking at outcomes (i.e. finding all organizations that had an increase in stock price of at least 10% in 2007 versus those that had 0% or negative returns) and then tracing backwards to the environmental/organizational factors that impacted them (a postdictive study). By far, the easiest way and fastest approach to applying linkage findings is by studying the organization at the current moment in time because there are many fewer variables to control.

The success of a concurrent study, examining an organization's results at a single point in time, is dependent on the existence of variance by organizational subunits on the responses to the survey items and other business performance metrics. If a survey is designed as a "feel-good" measure, or the response to an item is very favorably rated (e.g. safety or ethics), yielding uniformly positive results among the various organizational units, the ability to successfully perform linkage is reduced significantly.

The first step in a concurrent study is to obtain a one-to-one correspondence for each organizational unit for its survey results and its corresponding business performance metrics. If an organization has survey results for 100 units (departments, divisions, plants, stores, etc.), it should obtain the corresponding business performance metrics of relevance for those units. Those business metrics can be related to personnel issues, quality, production, sales, financial performance, etc., and could include measures such as voluntary turnover, sales per square foot, accident or injury rates, absenteeism, plant availability or uptime, production goal attainment, error rates, shrinkage, etc. The number and type of metrics that can be used are limited only by what is collected and relevant to the organization.

The correspondence between the survey results and the business metrics should be one-to-one with no overlap so that each observation or line of data (both survey and business metric) is mutually exclusive of the others, or orthogonal in nature. Imagine a retail chain with 100 stores. If either the customers shop at or the employees work at more than one of the stores, the one-to-one correspondence suffers. It may be better to perform the linkage not at the store, but at the regional level because it is much more likely that both employees and customers who may interact at numerous stores are more likely to stay within the region. The ideal case would be to have all employees only work in one store, to have all customers only shop in one store and to have other business metrics (turnover, shrink, etc.) cleanly measured store by store. It makes sense if you think of what the goal is—to determine which employee attitudes correspond to which customer perceptions or other business metrics.

It is often difficult to conduct linkage work across divisions of an organization in one study as the performance metrics, even when they are given similar or identical names, may be measuring different things or have different acceptable levels. A score on a particular metric of 75 in one division may be a very good score, and that same score on the same metric in a different division may be only average, compared to what could be achieved there. In other words, the same score can mean two different things across a broad piece of an organization, which will prevent successful linkage from being carried out. Conducting linkage with smaller pieces of the organization increases the likelihood that *a 75 is a 75 is a 75,* and that they all mean the same thing.

Many times when conducting linkage work, the greatest effort or amount of time spent is getting the data in order or understanding the elements in the data for the linkage study to be successfully completed.

Once the dataset is cleaned up and understood, the analyses can commence. The analyses used to study these "linked" datasets can be quite varied and can range from simple correlations to structured equation modeling to a whole host of other techniques to tease out meaning. Invariably the chicken and the egg question is raised. Do you need conditions that generate an excited, engaged workforce to obtain great business results? Or do great business results allow you to create conditions that excite and engage employees? The answer is that you need both because one does not exclusively cause the other, but because they feed off of each other in a reinforcing fashion. Some new research has demonstrated that attitudes have a bigger impact on performance over the longer term.

In the hundreds of linkage studies that I have reviewed or participated in, almost every time, the case can be made that certain employee attitudes can predict customer attitudes and other business performance metrics. In the few cases where it did not work, it is invariably due to the issues within the original dataset (i.e. what are called the same variables across an organization are actually being used to measure different things, the lack of mutually exclusive data points).

While linkage can be time consuming and difficult to conduct, it often yields extremely compelling information that can help guide an organization's decision making on which survey items to focus resources and attention on.

Organizational Diets

Thursday, July 26, 2007

Organizations

You want to lose weight? Eat less. It is that simple. Your weight is
a direct function of how many calories you take in each day against
how many calories you burn. Exercise, in addition to making critical
organs like the heart healthier, burns additional calories. If you eat
more calories than you burn, you gain weight. If you burn more
calories than you eat, you lose weight. It is within everyone's power
today, right now, to start losing weight. You do not need to spend a
dime on diet books, special supplements, sweat-inducing clothing,
large balls you can roll on, machines with rubber bands attached,
or a host of additional diet "aids." You simply need to take in
lower quantities of calories and you will lose weight. Yet if it is so
simple, why is there a multi-billion dollar industry aimed at helping
people lose weight? Can we not regulate our own bodies adequately,
adjusting our caloric intake to match the day's physical activity? Why
are we attracted to "get thin fast, eat all you want" promises? Want
a best selling book? Forget about the business book—there is no
money there. Write a diet book instead. The more outrageous the
claims in your diet book, the more likely you will make the best seller
list. If you really want to cash in on a book, write "Harry Potter's
Guide to Dieting: How Wizards Stay Supple."

While you can state that losing weight is simple—simply eating
less—the act of actually losing weight is not easy. We are not

programmed to simply eat less; we are programmed to get our calories when we can to help ensure our survival. That is the reason why high caloric foods tend to taste good. In more primitive times, with lean periods, those extra pounds might actually have saved your life. However, in our modern society, at least in some countries, lean periods with lower than needed caloric intake seem non-existent. *The FAO Statistical Yearbook* contains profiles on virtually every country in the world. From the USA profile, we see that between 1979 and 1981, the USA per capita potential average daily caloric intake was 3,180; from 1989 – 1991, it was 3,460; from 2001 – 2003, it was 3,770. These are huge numbers with a troubling trend and explain why there are so many overweight people in the United States. We simply have available to us and consume too many calories. Contrast this to a country like Zimbabwe, where the potential daily caloric intake from 2001 – 2003 was 2,010 per capita.

I just ran down to the kitchen and grabbed a bag of chocolate covered raisins—you have to get your fruit somewhere, right? In the nutritional facts section, it states that the estimated daily allowances that you get in a serving are based on a 2,000 calorie a day diet (your actual caloric needs may vary). We seem to be rapidly closing in on making available to each person almost two times their daily caloric needs based on the standards used by the chocolate raisin manufacturer.

Did our ancestors on the savannah worry about putting on a few extra pounds? They probably had more important things to worry about. I envision a conversation of two early proto-humans something like this: "Hey, ugh, you are looking a bit hefty around the middle. Are you eating too many starches? Not running after enough mastodons?" "Thanks, oog, you are looking a bit hefty yourself. Have you given up on that subsistence diet?"

Nanci Hellmich writing in *USA Today* (July 25, 2007) reports on a finding from the University of California that seems to suggest that "Obesity is Contagious." The findings state that "One person's obesity can significantly increase the chance that his or her friends, siblings and spouse also will become heavy, according to the first study done on how weight gain spreads through social networks. And if a person slims down, the people around him or her also may lose weight." While her writing may be a stretch of the word contagious, it seems that people who hang out together tend to impress on one another the social acceptability of various body types. In other words, when people hang out with overweight friends, being overweight is socially more acceptable.

If it was really this easy, all we would have to do is hang out with thin friends and we would all be thin. But with the United States population becoming "fatter" due to excessive calorie consumption, are we locked into a deleterious cycle since we are, by definition, hanging out with more overweight people?

All of this has interesting implications for organizations and organizational life. There are excessively "thin" organizations— organizations where resources are so limited that they are cutting into muscle, not fat, as they try to operate effectively with as little overhead and headcount as possible. These organizations run the risk of not growing effectively, or to the fullest extent as new opportunities arise, because there is absolutely no slack resources available.

There are also excessively "fat" organizations. Organizations can be "fat" by having excessive resources available, but I think they are more likely to achieve that designation by spending money on silliness and indulgences. Executives who install wood burning fireplaces in their mid-town offices come to mind, as do other headline-making indulgent occurrences. Being a thin organization is not bad, as Toyota's just-in-time manufacturing processes would attest, but being excessively thin can be a danger. It would be interesting to study Toyota's suppliers to see if they have become thin by hanging out with another thin organization. It may be that the only way you can be profitable when supplying a thin organization is by being thin yourself. I bet that many suppliers to Wal-Mart would attest to that.

Just as primitive people, as well as other animals, tended to grab their calories when they could find them, I don't know of an organization that does not grab its calories when it can find them as well. Oppositely, how many times have you heard someone say that they need to use up their budget because if they don't, they won't receive the same allocation for the next budget cycle. (We are really rewarding the right things, aren't we?) Remember that organizations are made up of people, people who do not magically leave their humanness at the door when they start a day at the "office." Those same qualities that make us susceptible to diet fads are at play in the office environment. As we all know, business fads (e.g. quality circles, business process re-engineering, t-groups, leaderless teams) come and go just about as fast as diet fads. The same attributes that make diet fads attractive are the characteristics that make business fads attractive. A business may be looking for a quick fix, a "get thin while eating all you want" business strategy. These strategies promise business success by adopting their simplistic rules, rules that will make you thin and attractive just like your neighbor (it will also help if you buy each of your managers a matching organizer and tote bag).

A contrarian viewpoint is that fads, however short lived, help to reinvigorate an organization by generating fresh ideas and getting people to try new things. However, fads also run a very big risk of jeopardizing employee views of organizational behavior and management effectiveness. Fads can be viewed as just one more thing that the organization undertakes which if employees "wait out," will simply fade away. After a few cycles, this creates a sense that management in the organization will latch onto quick fixes and the promise of easy solutions. Ultimately, this will cause employees to question the effectiveness and ability of the management team.

Unfortunately, business success takes a lot of "rolling up your sleeves" and sweating through the details, making long-term success independent of fads or organizational diets.

Reproductive Organizational Symbols

Saturday, April 7, 2007

Organizations

Like millions of other Americans before me, I was called for jury
duty last week. After three days of sitting for panels, I ended up
having my service deferred because the cases I was being considered
for were going to be lengthy, and I had previous commitments that I
could not rearrange. While I sat there, I thought about a few unique
things. I could not help but overhear multiple conversations where
people were griping about being called to serve. I have to admit,
I was not happy about it either, and I started thinking about the
causes of the resentment that seemed to well up from everyone in
the place—at least from the jurors. There were more police officers
walking around with guns than I have ever seen in one place before,
with the exception of the Yankees World Series game that I went to a
few years ago. I had to wonder if all the guns and law enforcers were
there in case any of the prisoners on trial attempted something or
whether they were there to keep the jurors in line.

Upon entering the Court House, there was a security screen much
like at the airport, manned by officers who really could learn a thing
or two about civility, courtesy and customer service from the TSA.
Protocols were in place that I was unused to, such as what was
required to take off or what was required to take out of a briefcase;
it did, however, look like the same security screening equipment that
the TSA uses. At the Court House, I could keep my shoes and jacket
on, but I had to take my watch and belt off, my wallet out of my

pocket. At LaGuardia Airport, I have to remove my jacket and shoes, but my watch, belt and wallet can stay on. If they are all looking for the same things, why aren't these machines used the same way? Are the screeners making it up as they go along?

You begin to wonder why the manufacturer of all this screening equipment didn't simply send directions on how to use it. I noticed that the vast majority of screeners were male. Given the widely-known male proclivity to ignore directions and to begin assembly of the things we buy (as men, we know the assembly information is built into our genes), I wondered if this is why all the security equipment operates differently—no one read the assembly or usage directions.

What really caught my attention at the Court House was the heavy use of organizational symbols. The place simply reeked of symbolism and protocol. Judges in robes, officers with badges and uniforms, lawyers and prisoners in suits. Somehow it was apropos that the lawyers and prisoners looked the same, though I think more often, the lawyers had slicked-back hair. Jurors, for the most part, were casually dressed. The symbolism went way beyond style of dress of course. There were mottos on the walls, statutes, heavy stone and cement construction symbolizing strength and durability— the reason why so many banks are built of brick or stone. Symbols were everywhere.

I could not help but wonder about the purpose of all these symbols. Would our criminal justice system dissolve if these symbols were not present? Would no one listen to the judge if he was not wearing a robe? (I personally found the three guys standing next to him with guns and following his orders motivational enough; I did not need his robe to let me know I should listen to him.) The whole legal system and its symbols seem built to intimidate, to play off our innate tendencies to yield to those in power. Are we seeing the struggle for power? A demonstration of who is in control, that the criminals have no power here, that it is the legal system in control? Is that what all this symbolism is there for?

I had to wonder if part of the resentment that most jurors seemed to feel partly sprang from having to relinquish established hierarchical relationships and routines in their day-to-day lives and to submit to new relationships and routines.

Certain situations magnify patterns of behavior that we see elsewhere; the Court System and its symbols is a magnifier of ordinary organizational life. Are organizations rife with symbols? You better believe it. The corner office, the executive dining room, the driver, the entourage are all symbols of executive power. Nine times out of ten, who is the last one to enter a room for a meeting? The executive can come last because it would be unseemly for the senior person to be sitting in a room waiting for others. After all, the executive is the most valuable person in the room and his/her time is precious. Not only was the judge the last person to enter the court room, but you had to stand when he entered. Would the proceedings have preceded any differently had we sat when he entered? I wonder. (I hope this doesn't give an executive out there any ideas.) Admittedly, not all executives have all these trappings or behave in this manner, but enough do to call it a pattern.

I can remember back to a job that I held years ago where I had succession information in my office and so my office had a lock. I was the only person at my level in this company whose office had a lock. I had to repeatedly explain to my peers why, and I found myself to be the victim of lock envy. When I went to the cafeteria for lunch, others would look at me and shy away, whispering under their breath, "he has a lock; he thinks he is better than us." To them, it was a symbol of status, and I have to admit that to me, it was a symbol that I was doing something important. I gave in to my primitive instincts—yes, it felt good that my door had a lock. It was an acknowledgement by the organizational powers that be that I counted. I will try not to fall off the wagon again.

Symbols, of course, are also all around us in everyday life and not just in our working environment. The backyard pool, the fancy car, the neighborhood you live in, the clothes you wear, along with a host of other material goods and behaviors, are all symbols of how you want others to perceive you.

Looking at all the symbols around us, part of me wants to laugh and I think, "Is this what we are really all about, seeing who can gather the most amount of symbolic accouterments around them?" Can we, as humans, move beyond these trivial symbols and see what is really important, or do we need these symbols for our society, as it is formed today, to function? Or is it even deeper than this? Are our brains hard-wired to recognize the power of symbols and do they help us organize societal life? Are we dependent on them?

Part of the answer may lie in looking beyond the human animal and examining other animals. Do they use symbols? Of course they do. The lion's mane, the coloring patterns in male birds, and bears and tigers, clawing and creating scratch marks on border trees to their territories—all symbols of intimidation or attraction, and sometimes both. This, however, raises an interesting question. Are the symbols of power and status found in organizational life really designed to show reproductive fitness to potential mates? Is the judge in his robe unconsciously saying I am more virile than the others in the room?

Is it as basic as all that? If so, we may never be able to get away from these symbols. I am not saying that organizational life is full of people who are eyeing each other continually as potential mates, but underneath it all, are we driven by basic instincts that cause us to behave in certain patterns? Patterns that maybe we just don't want to admit to ourselves, patterns that may cause discomfort? Did Freud have it right, at least partly? If we are to ever rise above being driven and controlled by symbols, the first step is an understanding of just what they are about and how they influence our day-to-day lives. Once you understand their power over you, you have a much better chance of controlling symbols, rather than letting them control you.

Oh, someone is knocking. I have to go and unlock the door.

Changing Times and Employee Engagement

Friday, December 14, 2007

Performance

What concerns organizations during times of change? Since organizations are nothing more than an amalgamation of people, organizations themselves actually have no concerns; however, people within those organizations, at differing levels, with differing responsibilities, can have widely differing concerns. And since organizations are made up of people, they have all of the foibles of people, the shortcomings that can become painfully obvious and even exaggerated during times of change.

Change, especially transformational change, is always spoken about in positive terms by an organization's management—who would want to implement change in order to make things worse than they are? Our goals are ones of improvement. Yet the act of change carries with it significant risk that the change will not work out and will instead degrade organizational performance. Depending on where you sit within the organization, your views toward change might be radically different. What may be viewed as a very successful change from the point of view of someone within finance may be viewed as a disaster from the point of view of a customer facing employee, struggling to meet customer needs.

Is there a way to ensure that everyone within the organization, or at least most, view the act and outcomes of change in the most positive light possible? If you can keep people engaged throughout the change process itself, the answer might just be "yes."

People are more similar than they are different with regard to the fundamental needs they look for work to fulfill, and the characteristics they desire from the working environment (I exclude those with psychopathology). These needs cut across industry, geography, ethnicity, gender, and generation, etc. They are uniform because underneath it all, we are all human. For instance, you would be hard pressed to find a worker anywhere on the planet who did not want to be treated with respect and dignity. Likewise, workers desire a sense of equity and in general, want to receive a fair return for the effort they expend. Workers also desire meaningfulness from what they are accomplishing; they want to have a sense of pride emanating from their efforts and pride in what their organization accomplishes. These are among the fundamentals that are part of who we are as human beings—and part of who we are comes from our evolution. Millions of years of evolution have created characteristics that are not erased simply because we have moved from the savannah to the suburbs, or simply because the younger generation has taken up snowboarding or freak dancing.

A worker in a developing country who submits to sweatshop-like or other horrible conditions does not accept those conditions because fundamentally he/she is any different from you or me. The worker accepts those conditions out of economic necessity. He/she has pressing needs that makes him/her accept conditions you or I would not *currently* tolerate—needs like feeding his/her family and putting a roof over their heads. If placed in circumstances with similar opportunities that you or I have, the worker would make the same choices that we would. Because these uniform fundamentals exist, there is a methodology that can be used to make organizational changes more positively viewed in general and to keep employees engaged during the process.

What about perceptions of differences by generation, by occupation, by public versus private sector employment, etc? Do these claims of uniformity fly in the face of the common wisdom—the common wisdom, for instance, that says that younger generation employees care less about job security than those of previous generations? No they do not. A younger generation employee who grew up during a period of high employment has less concern about job security because he/she simply has not experienced a time where unemployment was high. If unemployment soared to more than 10 percent, like it was when I was in college, this younger generation who does not care about job security would find that it is very important to him/her. The younger generation worker is not fundamentally different than previous generations; he/she simply has had different experiences and economic opportunities available.

Let's examine a case where among other things, the equity equation got out of balance and engagement declined. As reported in the *Wall Street Journal* (February 9, 2007), prior to 9/11, the U.S. Air Marshal Service had 33 agents covering 26,000 flights. After 9/11, in an effort to beef up airline security, it was decided that somewhere between 2,500 and 4,000 new Air Marshalls were to be hired (the exact number is classified). Two hundred thousand people applied for these new positions. The number of applicants can be surmised to be so high because people were feeling a sense of patriotism after 9/11 and a desire to do something to be of service to their country. They came into these jobs excited about the prospect of doing something meaningful and with a strong desire to do a good job. They did not take these jobs expecting extraordinarily high wages— fair wages would suffice. After joining the Service, they found themselves faced with what has been described as grueling schedules, a lack of advancement, onerous rules affecting their ability to their get jobs done, and a lack of identity protection, resulting in "many" (in the words of other Marshalls) quitting the Service—the ultimate act of a disengaged workforce.

The head of the Service at the time called these complainers "disgruntled amateurs, insurgents and organizational terrorists." I don't know about you, but I get the feeling that calling individuals who joined the U.S. Air Marshalls after 9/11 *organizational terrorists* is probably the worst thing you could call them. With the work situation, including the equity equation, being out of balance, the Marshalls responded to these working conditions by joining a union. The head of the Air Marshall's Service has since been replaced and the new head has begun to make changes such as loosening the dress code so the Air Marshalls blend in better with other passengers and taking other steps to protect their identities. Clearly the change that the U.S. Air Marshall Service undertook, that of vastly expanding its ranks and providing additional security on airline flights, cannot yet be called a complete success story.

Just as aspects of organizational culture are not binary conditions, the success or failure of change and people's concerns about it should not be viewed as binary either. In other words, people are not either concerned or unconcerned, change is not either successful or unsuccessful and employees are not either engaged or disengaged. Treating and speaking about such concepts in a binary fashion is far too simplistic. Change and concerns about it fall along a continuum. The degree of concern regarding change can vary from a great deal of concern to no concern, depending on the individual, and the change itself can be viewed as a ranging from complete success to complete failure.

The fundamentals of creating a work environment where change can be positively implemented and employees engaged can be depicted in the Message Performance Future (MPF) model, which has been successfully used in describing organizational culture and working through change.

Message: Is there absolute clarity regarding what the organization is about, how it will operate and how each person contributes to delivering on those goals? Importantly, are the organizational communications delivering the Message consistent throughout all the levels of the organization? Are policies and practices in line with that Message? During times of change, is it clear how the organization is changing, what the expected benefits of the change will be and what each person's role in the change effort is?

Performance: Are people getting what they need (in the broadest sense) to be able to deliver on that Message—to get the job done? U.S. Air Marshalls who could not blend in with the other passengers were handicapped in their ability to deliver on the Message, to provide increased security on flights. Performance should be thought of in the broadest sense, including such areas as teamwork, communications, decision making, training, equipment, resources, processes and procedures.

Future: Do people feel like they have a Future and a sense of belonging, of being valued by the organization? Is there a reason for them to stick around for the long-term?

As stated earlier, organizational cultures are not binary, and every organization will have varying degrees of each being present. The most successful organizations at implementing change and keeping employees engaged during change are those that are strong in all three areas. For instance, one client had some employees who viewed the organization positively in all three areas, and as an outcome, that group had engagement scores in the mid 80s (on a percent favorable scale of 1–100). Within the same client, those who did not view the organization as offering a clear Message, as providing what is needed to get the job done (Performance) and a sense of Future had engagement scores in the low teens. Ensuring that Messages about the change process are sent out regularly and consistently, including communication on people's roles during and after the change, is critical. This is also true in providing people what they need to Perform and giving people a sense of Future after the change.

Sometimes change efforts impacting mission critical processes or change efforts involving critical processes can carry terrible consequences if the change effort was to fail. For example, failure of a change process is often not an option, especially when that process is one that protects the public's safety or puts the life of an employee at risk. In those cases, a change process that has multiple small steps with assurance check points along the way, which confirm the change is working, can be done. Another approach is to implement the change in an off-line fashion, running two processes in parallel, and not to implement the change in the "real-world" until it is assured that the newly changed process is functioning as planned.

Change is a never ending state of being because there is no such thing as a perfect organization—only a vision of perfection that one can strive for only to find that it is constantly somewhat out of reach.

Behavior Attitude or Attitude Behavior

Monday, January 21, 2008

Performance

One consulting project took place in a very remote corner of Southeast Asia. We were there to conduct an employee survey that aimed to improve organizational effectiveness. There were several thousand employees at this remote location and the employee base was a mixture of local tribes, tribes from other parts of Southeast Asia and American expatriates. This location was probably the closest I would ever come to living in a small American town circa 1950, as the company had reproduced a facsimile complete with schools, bowling alleys, grocery stores an infirmary, theater, golf course and barber shop with a stripped pole in front, country club with Olympic sized pool and cafeteria/mess hall. There was street after palm-tree-lined-street of bungalows in which families lived and there were guest bungalows for visitors. Each bungalow had a screened-in front porch in which you could rock in comfortable wicker chairs as the day ended, cooling off and watching the world go by. There was also a hotel for short-term visitors that reminded me of the days of Howard Johnson or Holiday Inn drive-up-to-your-door places. The location was immaculate with a large gardening staff who maintained the grounds, trimming the fast growing tropical plants that seemed to thrive in the hot humid conditions, and in general, kept things in top form. Occasionally a troop of monkeys could be seen meandering through a neighborhood.

The quaint, perfect American dream right? Well, just as in the 1950s, the American dream was not so perfect; underneath the surface, this place was not paradise for a number of its residents either. As it turned out, the pool was used for "certain" residents on certain days, segregated by occupational level, which was also strongly related to which tribe you were from. The mess hall had a cinder block wall about two feet high running down the center. One side was carpeted; the other cement, and just like the pool, certain groups were relegated to certain sides. (The food available to everyone was identical). Other conditions hinting at class distinctions abounded, seemingly driven to some extent by tribal affiliation. I made several friendships that I still cherish today, but I was taken aback on more than one occasion when a local would give me some friendly advice about not getting too close to specific people. The local would say that my new friends had come from a group that was cannibalistic as little as 20 years ago. The previously cannibalistic tribe was at the bottom of the social structure. I developed a good friendship with one member of this tribe and I heard many jokes made at his expense about being careful if he wanted to have me over for dinner.

As part of my work to understand this organization, and to help develop the appropriate questions to use in an employee survey aimed at improving effectiveness, I along with my team, conducted focus groups with people from all areas and occupational levels of the company. To reach some of the focus groups, I vividly remember taking a ride in a Vietnam-era Huey helicopter with no doors. During the ride, I gazed at mile after mile of palm-oil plantations, covering a vast area that used to be tropical rain-forest. In general, during the focus groups there was little to no mention of the class system that had developed in the organization. When I discussed this with the American expatriates, who were generally in management or very technical positions, they told me that advice given to them (typically given by locals residing at the top of the social ladder) on sustaining a harmonious environment was to allow the class distinctions to flourish—don't rock the boat, the standards by which all employees expected this game to be played. Except it was not a game, it was real life. These standards had become ingrained enough that they were not often mentioned in discussions for improving organizational performance. It did not seem to occur to employees that the social structure was something that could change.

I was in a bit of a quandary. I was retained to work on organization effectiveness. Should I have tried to improve the organization within the parameters, the conditions that the workers had set and were used to? Or should I have tried to impose my own standards of conduct and attitudes that had developed from my own background? Did I have any right to try to impose my own convictions on others? And should I attempt to gather the data from the survey, using the data as a lever to try to change attitudes, how various groups perceive themselves being treated, or should I immediately suggest some changes in behavior? The immediate decision revolved around which approach would have more impact—trying to change some attitudes and with that, some resultant behaviors, or should I try to immediately change some behaviors?

What comes first? Do attitudinal shifts lead to changes in behavior or can you have more of an impact on attitudes if you first change behavior? It was very clear to me that many managers were uncomfortable with the current situation, but were unsure how best to proceed. They were charged with the operation of a major installation for their company and not necessarily social engineering in a land and culture in which many of them were strangers. Could an argument be made that even though this operation was very successful, further success and efficiencies could be gained by beginning to change the social structures by which they operated? But again, how should that be approached—through educational efforts aimed at changing attitudes or by going directly for behavior change?

We began with a little of both. First, we put together a survey taskforce that consisted of about 50 people. While this was many more people than we needed, it allowed us to reach out to people from all areas of the company and to people with a diversity of backgrounds. We spent weeks over the course of the project with this group having them work together to accomplish jointly held goals, so that they got to know each other better. They were empowered to make decisions and they drove the project; we simply advised along the way. Management also did away with the regulations at the swimming pool; the wall in the cafeteria was torn down and the entire place was made to look uniform. Superficial? Yes, but it was a start.

If you can get people to immediately start behaving differently in their day-to-day interactions with others, this will support your efforts around attitude change. And if you can change attitudes, behavior change (or additional behavior changes) can be easier to accomplish. If you don't work on the attitudes though, even with changes in behavior, eventually the old behaviors will reassert themselves. And if all you do is work on attitudes without corresponding changes in behaviors, the old attitudes are reinforced by the undesirable behaviors. We made a conscious decision to attack both the behaviors immediately, and through the use of the survey/feedback tool, we focused on the attitudes and additional behaviors to modify the way this organization operated.

This project was repeated three times over the course of four to five years and each time, actions were taken to improve organizational performance (e.g. the organization moved from a centralized support structure to a decentralized one more in tune with its geographic dispersion).

During each iteration of the project, a different group of 50 project coordinators were chosen to help implement, striving for a large impact on people that we directly touched. Each manager receiving results received extensive training on discussing the results with his/her respective staffs and on change implementation to provide assistance to those whom we only indirectly touched. The implementation team tracked the actions and assisted managers with their efforts. At the end of that time, the organization apparently was pleased with the changes that had been wrought.

Were imbedded prejudices or class distinctions erased by what we accomplished for this organization? I think it was unlikely that in the period we were working there, we made lasting fundamental changes. However, did we move the dial a bit in the positive direction for this organization and the people living within? I certainly hope so.

Organizational Aliens

Thursday, February 22, 2007

Performance

There are people who believe that some of the ancient wonders
of the world, such as the Egyptian pyramids or Stonehenge, could
not possibly have been built by "primitive" man; the pieces of
stone were too massive, the joints too perfect, the engineering far
too complex for early man to have done this unaided. Some of
these structures are lined up to predict the turnings of the seasons,
marking the summer or winter solstice, are lined up to "true" north,
or have dimensions that were developed according to the golden
ratio in order to achieve an aesthetically pleasing design; feats that
seem impossible to many of us today because many of us personally
would have no idea how to accomplish them. Therefore, how could
early or primitive man?

Some have gone so far as to point to these feats as "proof" of
past alien visits to the Earth to assist us on the path to civilization.
These beliefs often simply uncover our own ignorance and can be
made when people equate early man with primitive or a lack of
intelligence. While I may question the intelligence of man, given
some of the things as a species we have done, such as despoiling our
environment, our current level of intelligence has been with us since
Homo sapiens appeared. Just as it is a mistake to underestimate the
intelligence of your adversaries, it is a mistake to underestimate the
intelligence of early man. As humans, when we set out to accomplish
something, and put our minds behind it, we can accomplish quite a bit.

A question I have asked is, "how do excellent organizations arise?" Assume for a moment that we can agree on the definition of an excellent organization. The question is, does humankind have the ability to create a Google type organization on our own? Alternatively, will the creation of Google, as well as some other excellent organizations, be pointed to by some future generation as further evidence of alien visitations? Organizational aliens who came to Earth to show us the way toward organizational improvement? Are Larry Page and Sergey Brin really of this planet or are they here just to help us get on our feet?

The Rare Earth Hypothesis states that the life on Earth arose due to an extremely rare combination of events—one in a billion or more. If you believe in the Rare Earth hypothesis, life in the universe would be very uncommon, occurring only very occasionally. The principle of mediocrity is just the opposite. It states that the Earth is nothing special. It is a typical rocky planet, revolving around an average star, located in the Milky Way, an average galaxy. In addition, if you believe in that hypothesis, life in the universe would be much more likely to arise on multiple planets.

If we use those analogies to think about the rise of excellent organizations, are they more like the Rare Organizational Hypothesis—excellent organization arise due to an extremely rare combination of events (i.e. very profitable, dominates industry segment, changes the paradigm), and hence, come along just every great once in a while? Alternatively, are they more like the principle of mediocrity (possibly a poor choice of labels), whereby every organization has within it the potential to become truly excellent? All we need to do is unlock the potential.

When previously asked, "what do I get out of my work, what do I find rewarding?" My response has been consistent. I work with organizations that tend to have relatively large numbers of employees. Through my work, I strive to make the organization a more effective, a more efficient place. At the same time, if I can make the work environment 10% or 15% better for the people who work in that environment, I feel that I have done my part, if not to improve the whole world, then to improve the piece of it that I can touch.

Somehow, deep inside, I find that answer is not good enough. I want to push myself to the edge. I want to create and be part of excellent organizations. I don't want to just go along for the ride; I want to be part of something special. I want to be able to point to a lasting artifact, a pyramid and say I had a hand in that. For that to come true, I am rooting for the principle of mediocrity (that true excellence can be common), and that what we need to do is unlock the potential that is deep inside all organizations.

However, there is a warning sign waving out there. It is the Fermi Paradox. It states that if alien life is common, given the age of the universe, we should not have to look very hard to find them. Homo sapiens have been building organizations for a very long time. How easy it is to find truly excellent ones?

CAN YOU FEEL THE MUSIC?

THURSDAY, DECEMBER 27, 2007

PERFORMANCE

> *"Remember when the music came from wooden boxes strung with silver wire*
> *And as we sang the words, it would set our minds on fire,*
> *For we believed in things, and so we'd sing."*
> *—Harry Chapin, Remember When the Music*

Sometimes I wonder what it means that many of the musicians that I really like are dead. Poets, musicians and other artists sometimes have incredible insights into what we are as a species. The refrain from the song above "And as we sang the words, it would set our minds on fire" might be quite literally correct if not simply artistically correct. Music, and the emotions that it can stir, plays an incredibly important part in the human makeup. Some music can literally drive you to tears, evoke warm and wonderful memories, stir the spiritual side in us or bring forth nationalistic tendencies. When I am driving my small convertible, there is nothing quite like ZZ Top songs, "Born to Run" by Bruce Springsteen or "Hotel California" by the Eagles to make the time fly (and hopefully not lead to a speeding ticket).

Some insight into music's place in our brain is made more evident by stories about people who are ill or have had an accident that affects their relationship to music. Oliver Sachs, the noted neurologist, author and educator, in his book "Musicophila," describes a man who had no particular affinity out of the ordinary for music, but a few weeks after being struck by lightning, developed an incredible urge to listen to and write piano music. While the etiology of the change is unknown, the man described events and memories from the strike that led Sacks to state that the emotional parts of the brain, the amygdala, the cortex and the brainstem may have been involved. He further speculates that the lightening strike may have set off temporal lobe seizures. This short circuiting may have affected the higher functioning centers of the brain like the cortex (responsible for self, language, thought, consciousness, memory etc.) and the core components of the brain like the amygdala where emotions seem to germinate and the brainstem responsible for autonomic functions like respiration, sweating and maintaining homeostasis in the body. In other words, the higher order functions of his brain were put more directly in touch (my speculation) with the basic core components of the brain and the result was an urge to listen to and create music. Is that a reason why music is sometimes so powerful, so moving, because it more directly connects our higher centers of thought processing with our elemental core components—a sensation that many of us might find pleasurable?

You can learn something about this by not only looking at "normal" people who develop issues, but by also examining the other end of the continuum—"abnormal" people and how the issue around music might play out with them. Paul Babiak and Robert Hare are the authors of "Snakes in Suits, When Psychopaths go to Work." A psychopathic person is someone without conscience, unable to empathize with others (seeing things from another's perspective or understand another's feelings), incapable of guilt, and are loyal only to themselves. As a group, they are responsible for some of the more horrific crimes that are described in the media. This group is unable to show any remorse for its actions because it lacks the ability to be remorseful. Significant portions of those in prison are psychopathic.

In addition, while many of us may not be surprised that there are psychopaths in prison, we may be somewhat more surprised by some studies that suggest that psychopaths are also found in corporations. The authors repeatedly warn in their book that just because an individual may exhibit a single characteristic that could be labeled psychopathic, without a whole series of other corroborating psychopathic characteristics, you are in all likelihood not dealing with a psychopath. However, one study of corporate managers in the UK stated that 3.5% were psychopaths compared to 1% in the general population. There is currently no effective treatment for psychopathy.

Hare states in an interview with *Fast Company* (July 2005), "There are certainly more people in the business world who would score high in the psychopathic dimension than in the general population. You'll find them in any organization where, by the nature of one's position, you have power and control over other people and the opportunity to get something." Babiak as a rationale states, "The psychopath has no difficulty dealing with the consequences of rapid change; in fact, he or she thrives on it. Organizational chaos provides both the necessary stimulation for psychopathic thrill seeking and sufficient cover for psychopathic manipulation and abusive behavior." Entrepreneurs almost by definition are not psychopathic. Entrepreneurs want to build, want to create something that outlasts themselves, psychopaths tend to take advantage of and abuse what already exists.

A quote from Babiak and Hare's book stood out, "Some researchers have commented that psychopaths 'know the words but not the music,' a statement that accurately captures their cold and empty core." Therefore, from Sach's work, we now have a situation in which the brain, when injured, has some of the higher thought processing areas more in touch, better connected with the emotional core, the result is a desire to listen to, or create music (some experience musical hallucinations). In addition, from Babiak and Hare, the notion that psychopaths (including those at work) do not seem capable of connecting their higher thought processes with the understanding that an emotional component brings, often times at great detriment to the organization or society as a whole.

I have to wonder, and I have seen some research that confirms this, that one marker of psychopathy would be people who when shown disturbing pictures can process the content intellectually, but an electroencephalograph (EEG) of the brain would show a lack of response in the emotional centers of the brain. They were born or due to injury or other circumstance with their emotional centers of the brain somewhat detached from the higher thought processing centers. In addition, of course, this condition would not be binary, but rather would reside along a continuum, meaning that being psychopathic is not necessarily an all or nothing condition. Like almost all other things that affect humans, it comes in varying degrees. At some point, the person would be far enough away from the average to be considered pathological. Another thought crossed my mind, "Do psychopaths enjoy music as much as the rest of us?" Psychopaths certainly can create or listen to music; Charles Manson for instance who is certainly psychopathic, was an aspiring musician prior to the Tate-LaBianca murders by the Manson cult, but was there any enjoyment, any emotional connection by him out of the musical experience? My guess is that it is unlikely.

Some managers can be emotionally challenged, lacking empathy or the ability to see things from the perspectives of others—they literally do not understand the pain they may be causing others or may view it as a necessary condition for the businesses to function or thrive. (This does not mean that they are psychopaths). They may understand the business consequences of their actions, but are unable to understand the emotional impact on those affected.

While I don't think of it as a particularly rare case, I remember that a number of years ago, I had a senior manager, prior to doing a really terrible thing within his organization, describe to me what he was about to do as "just business" and had to be done because of, from his perspective, "lost opportunity." His actions would disrupt and possibly destroy the lives of many employees. He showed only a surface level of concern to those that would be affected by this event. The "just business" component of the rationale may have been a rationalization within his own head to justify how he could do what he was about to, or it could indicate a real lack of ability to emote with others, a lack of conscience, and a lack of loyalty to those so affected. On the surface what may appear to be a lack of ethics, may actually indicate a deeper pathological illness. I wondered if after the event whether this particular manager felt any remorse, or guilt. My guess is that he did not. In addition, while it is unlikely that this particular manager was psychopathic, he was certainly emotionally challenged, most likely narcissistic, and unable to understand how others would "feel."

"It is just business." Is that a rationale that should be rewarded? The investment community seems to cheer at times when callous leaders are put into place to shake up an organization. Do you remember what Al "Chainsaw" Dunlap did to Sunbeam or Scott Paper? (His lack of emotion may be epitomized by the fact that he did not attend either of his parent's funerals). How about what Paul Bilzerian did to The Singer Company? (He is also known for serving time in prison on charges of corporate fraud.) Did the "Queen of Mean," Leona Helmsley deserve the title for being emotionally disconnected from her employees or was she simply misunderstood? (She was so emotionally unattached to other humans that she left millions to her dog—the dog being one of the few who she felt stood by her). In addition, of course, there is the litany of more current plunderers by executives at places like Enron and WorldCom. Did the executives of those organizations feel remorse or guilt at the employees who lost their life savings or retirement pensions? Is it "just business," or is it something more than that, maybe something more sinister?

It has been a very long time since I worked in employee selection. In my rather limited, dated knowledge of employee selection, I wonder if anyone has looked at musicality as selection criteria (not for just musicians). Would there be a benefit in evaluating a candidate on whether he/she can emotionally connect to music? Rather abstract, and there are certainly more direct ways and more conventional ways to measure psychopathy or other emotional issues, but nevertheless the results of a study in this area would be fascinating and would potentially tell us a lot more about who we are.

There are some terrific work places out there. All sorts of places strive to be on the "best of this or that list." It would be interesting to evaluate a list of some of the best places for the role that music plays in the work environment. An organization where people literally "whistle while you work" may be a signpost of an emotionally healthy workplace, one where the environment has been created that allows people to connect their higher thought processes with their emotional cores. A common phrase, "this place really hums" or a manager stating that "this place can really sing." These simple phrases may be taping into a very deep construct embedded into the very wiring of our brains and be intimately connected with our emotions.

Swarming as a Business Model

Wednesday, January 16, 2008

Organizations

"Five Iranian Revolutionary Guard boats 'harassed and provoked' three U.S. Navy ships early Sunday in international waters, the U.S. military said Monday, calling the encounter a 'significant' confrontation." (CNN, January 7, 2008) The three U.S. ships, a guided missile destroyer, a guided missile frigate and a guided missile cruiser were harassed by five small speedboats who got as close as 200 yards (incredibly), dropped objects into the ship's paths, forcing them to take evasive action and supposedly made threatening pronouncements via the radio. The U.S. ships were about to use high powered large caliber machine guns, which can shoot 10 rounds per second, to defend themselves just as the Iranians broke off.

Were these big, powerful, state-of-the-art U.S. Navy warships ever really threatened by these small speedboats? Should this be dismissed as a swarm of gnats would be to an elephant or is this approach, a group of small ships attacking a much larger adversary, something to note?

While five Iranian speedboats don't exactly make up a swarm, this may have been a dry run for a tactic they could use should a military confrontation occur. As we all know, swarming insects such as bees and ants often successfully attack and kill much larger animals. In many cases, while many individual members perish in these attacks, the large number of members defending or attacking yields eventual success to the swarm.

Other social animals that hunt in packs such as lions, hyenas and wolves are able to bring down prey much larger then themselves. They leverage the resources of a hunting party made up of many discrete units working in a coordinated fashion toward a common goal. Dolphins and whales near the top of the food chain, working in unison will herd schools of fish into a tighter and tighter ball and then make passes through the swarm to fill their stomachs. One swarm of nimble predators, even though of larger size, outmaneuvers another swarm of smaller fast moving fish. The fish swarmed seeking safety in numbers and the whales and dolphins, using their social structure, figured out how to use the swarm against itself by forcing it into a small tight ball where they could grab mouthfuls of sustenance. Members of the hunting party keep the fish tightly herded while others take turns feeding.

In 2002, a military war game had small, fast moving speedboats inflict great damage on a U.S. military flotilla. "In that war game, the Blue Team navy, representing the United States, lost 16 major warships—an aircraft carrier, cruisers and amphibious vessels—when they were sunk to the bottom of the Persian Gulf in an attack that included swarming tactics by enemy speedboats. The sheer numbers involved overloaded their ability, both mentally and electronically, to handle the attack. The whole thing was over in five, maybe 10 minutes" (*The New York Times*, January 12, 2008). The now retired commander of the exercise indicated frustration that at the time, the Navy did not widely embrace the startling findings of this exercise and prepare for this new version of asymmetrical warfare at sea. The

Navy is now taking notice. I hope that it will figure out how to react like the dolphins and whales using the swarm against itself to its own advantage, resulting in a successful outcome.

"Swarming is a seemingly amorphous but carefully structured, coordinated way to strike from all directions at a particular point or points, by means of a sustainable 'pulsing' of force and/or fire, close-in as well as from stand-off positions. It will work best perhaps only, if it is designed mainly around the deployment of myriad small, dispersed, networked maneuver units. The aim is to coalesce rapidly and stealthily on a target, attack, then dissever and redisperse, immediately ready to recombine for a new pulse. Unlike previous military practice, battle management is now mainly about 'command and decontrol,' as networked units all over the field of battle (or business, or activism, or terror and crime) coordinate and strike the adversary in fluid, flexible, nonlinear ways" (Rand Corporation).

What about business organizations? Are there any lessons to be learned from these events or from the swarming methodology that can be applied or tested? One approach to swarming in business would be to have flexible, small units with increased information flows effectively pulling together dispersed action oriented groups to achieve a common objective. They would disband as quickly as they formed, and rapidly prepare to come together potentially with the same or different components of the organization to achieve the next objective, with a nimbleness and impact that a large lumbering organization would have difficulty matching. Would these tactics provide a competitive advantage or would it simply be the latest and greatest fad to fade away as the effort to implement was found to outweigh the potential benefit? Do smaller organizations benefit from using the swarming methodology, or can larger organizations also apply these techniques successfully and to a competitive advantage?

While there are potentially numerous ways to utilize these techniques (and each is likely to have drawbacks as well as benefits), some challenges seem to more readily lend themselves to this swarming approach than others. For instance, when project teams execute on critical activities for the organization (such as setting up a skunk works for new product or process development) or for its customers, being able to call upon small flexible groups, which represent the best and the brightest, may create additional potential, not available from larger more static organizations. Sales organizations may find swarming advantageous when trying to land new clients or renewing existing relationships. Marketing may find swarming, getting the word out about products or services, through multiple channels using smaller, less costly efforts advantageous to one large expensive effort that once over has depleted marketing resources or budget. Swarming may also be advantageous for problem resolution efforts. Some of the these swarming applications are obvious, but are there other potential uses?

There are business applications that already take advantage of the concept of swarming or variations thereof and there are others on the way. One of the benefits of swarming from a business standpoint is the elimination of single "mission critical" pinch points, which allow multiple redundancies to be built in creating systems that are more robust. With many small flexible components coming together, if one component is unable to participate in completing its objectives, another similar component can step into the breach and the final goal is still achieved.

Take for instance "cloud computing." If Google has its way, we will all become part of cloud computing in the near future. Cloud computing is in essence the elimination of your personal PC as the keeper of your applications and data. Instead of residing on your workstation or on an application server, they reside in a "cloud" of computers—multiple computers that can direct their resources to where they are currently needed (swarming)—that can be accessed from any portal in the world. Instead of lugging your PC, you would simply sign onto your virtual PC from any portal and all of your applications and data would be immediately accessible. If the portal in your house broke, you would simply put in a new one and sign on to your application and data. You could sign on from a hotel room, from a client, from the airport, from your car or at work at multiple locations and all of your information would be there along with the applications you use still setup the way you desire.

Let's speculate about what aspects of "Cloud HR" might look like. One aspect could be the notion that individual companies do not have their own internal systems to run their respective HR processes, but rather, they would signup belonging as members to a comprehensive HR system/service shared by many organizations. This comprehensive system and service provider would not exist on a single server/system or even necessarily be represented by the resources that a single service provider could bring to bear, but rather would reside in the "cloud" of computers or the "cloud" of companies providing the service. This cloud provides multiple redundancies in case of the failure of any one component and allows resources to be directed to where it is most needed moment by moment by the member companies. The cloud could be coordinated by an integrating component, an organization with that specific task, which figures out which resources to direct where to attain maximal performance for the cloud members.

If the system was a computer-based system, upon signing onto the system, the administrator or end-user would get the configured version of the system tailored to his or her own particular environment. One benefit of this approach would be cost sharing across the user set for upgrades to the system. Other "shared" services provided by the "cloud" could include any HR services where advantage could be gained from accepting, temporarily as needed, services from a provider able to rapidly bring together project teams or to focus resources on issues that member organizations needed resolved and could include various employee life-cycle services such as recruiting, selection, onboarding, retention, etc. From a service standpoint, swarming would be accomplished by having multiple interchangeable sites proving uniform services according to an agreed upon standard in a coordinated fashion rather than the reliance on single-source or mega-site locations.

The HR, marketing and sales departments are not the only departments that could potentially benefit from the swarming methodology. One could imagine with the advent of truly flexible manufacturing facilities that organizations could "share" capacity calling upon capabilities and resources as required and realizing potential cost savings during slower periods.

Traditional businesses are not the only potential beneficiaries from this approach. For instance, encyclopedias used to be complied by a small pool of noted scholars on each topic (or for lower budget encyclopedias someone who simply knew something about the topic). Wikipedias use a similar approach to the military's "command and decontrol. The way a swarm of individuals contribute their respective knowledge about a topic is transforming the way we think of reference material, the collection of knowledge, creating a new norm. Wikipedia is developing processes to ensure that the swarm produces not only various points of view on a topic, but also a high quality product.

While some of what can be thought of in terms of the application of a swarming methodology can be pretty far out there, other possibilities are much more present in the here and now and are waiting to be applied by various kinds of organizations—including, unfortunately, some potential adversaries.

Classification of Organizational Behaviors—The Oy Definitions and Behaviors

Sunday, July 27, 2008

Just for Kicks

I was trying a new program and was analyzing some organizational data. As I looked across a large number of organizations, some organizational attribute patterns emerged. The new program had some strange properties and it seemed to come up with some unusual categorizations. Here you go.

- K'nocker Organization—too big for its britches, a big shot organization

- Kvetching Organization—always complaining about market conditions or execution or pricing power or…just always kvetching

- The Fars Organizations—Fartootst, Farmisht, Farchadat— essentially, mixed up and confused

- Schlemiel Organization—simpleton, not sophisticated in its thinking

- Schnozzle Organization—can smell which way the wind is blowing and is aware of changing market conditions. Sometimes shortened to the Schnoz Organization

- Schtarker Organization—strong, successful, to the point of boastfulness

- Chutzpah Organization—willing to tell its customers that it knows better than they do

- Schmoozing Organization—has an emphasis on marketing

- Schmaltzy Organization—fancy, literally dripping with fat (meaning fanciness)

- Tchotchkes Organization—likes to produce little tokens for customers to help them remember the organization

- Schpritzing Organization—has a very high workload, and everyone walks around sweating

- Schlimazel Organization—can't execute, can't get things right

- Schmegegge Organization—focused on petty issues; can't see big picture

- Schmatte Organization—literally rags or a piece of cloth; tries to get by on a shoe string, everyone works with shmattes

- Schmeer Organization—spreads everyone really thin, trying to cover multiple tasks

- Kosher Organization—one where everything is ok

- Traf Organization—opposite end of the kosher scale

- Tzadaka Organization—righteous, operates with very high integrity and is generous with its success

- Bupkes Organization—literally "beans and goat turds," gives nothing to it employees or customers

- Dreck Organization—producer of low quality goods and services

- Dybbuk Organization—condemned to wander aimlessly between small profits and small losses, not growing and never able to accomplish anything because of its sins

- Golem Organization—superstitious, thinks it can create new job families, made out of mud and sticks, to solve its problems

- Chelm Organization—populated by simpletons and fools

- Bubeleh Organization—a term of affection, an organization that is spoken of fondly

- Yenta Organization—gossip and the rumor mill are very strong here

- Tsedrayt Organization—lacks a clear mission or goals

- Tsuris Organization—gives everyone grief, aggravation and trouble

- Klutz Organization—where much rework is
  stumbled through

- Nebbish Organization—a decision is never made, or if
  made will likely be changed, maybe

- Noshing Organization—one where every meeting is
  accompanied by food

- Mamaloshen Organization—makes up its own "mother
  tongue," makes heavy use of acronyms and other
  made-up words

- Mentsch Organization—honorable and decent, an
  organization filled with good people

- Maven Organization—leading edge science and processes,
  expert, authority

- Toches ahfen tish Organization—accountability is
  high (literally your rear-end is on the table)

- Toches-lecker Organization—everyone is managing upward,
  a brown-noser organization

- Schlepping Organization—doesn't have enough chairs and
  everyone is schlepping chairs from room to room when
  there is a meeting

- *Oy—a Yiddish exclamation of exasperation often used as one moves
  chairs from room to room*

Putting on the Farpitz—
The Oy Definitions and Behaviors—
Part 2

Sunday, August 1, 2008

Just for Kicks

The response has been overwhelming to the last posting (chapter) with many suggestions for additional words and behavioral definitions. So one last time, here is Part 2 of the Oy Definitions incorporating many of those suggestions except for the vulgar ones, (even if they don't sound vulgar in Yiddish) and I promise to stop after this.

- Alter Cocker Organization—an organization (often more mature) that is set in its ways and unwilling to adopt new ideas. This organization is sometimes seen with its pants pulled up well above the waistline, wears white tank top undershirts and occasionally smokes cigars while making threatening gestures to the kids playing in the street.

- Farpitz Organization—an organization where appearance is very important and everyone gets dressed up every day is said to be farpitz or dressed fancy. I think I heard from a hairdresser that appeared on Oprah who said they heard from a friend that Gene Wilder's dance routine with Frankenstein was originally called Putting on the Farpitz, but was edited down to Putting on the Ritz.

- Haymish Organization—is a warm, friendly organization where people feel comfortable. Usually somehow incorporates eating food

- Chazerei Organization—one that serves bad food

- Fershtinkiner Organization—what the organization smells like after everyone eats the really bad food

- Kibitzing Organization—is one that always has something to say, even when it doesn't

- Kishka Organization—rather than a type of organization, this is the guts of the organization, where the work is done. When you reach down into the bowels of the organization, into the trenches, those are the kishkas of the organization. If you punch an organization in the kishkas, it really hurts.

- Kvelling Organization—when everyone in an organization is beaming with pride, it is a kvelling organization.

- Luftmensh Organization—an organization with lofty unrealistic goals is called a luftmensh organization; its head is in the clouds

- Macher Organization—an ambitious organization dominating its industry with many schemes and plans

- Meshugge Organization—a crazy organization where people view the decisions being made as totally meshugge or not making sense

- Mishpoca Organization—an organization that views its employees as part of the family, giving it a warm inviting feeling

- Mohel (Moyle) Organization—an organization that is always cutting back. More could be said here, but less may be better

- Naches Organization—when a subsidiary or division beats its forecasts and makes the parent organization or corporate HQ really feel good about its achievements. That parent organization is full of Naches

- Pisher Organization—a young inexperienced organization (with bladder control issues) is a pisher of an organization. Ben and Jerry's (against my advice) was contemplating turning this into an ice cream flavor, a lemony colored Pish Food, but to be acceptable added an "h" and some chocolate and marshmallow and turned it into Phish Food

- Momzer Organization—one that is not worthy of trust

- Noodge Organization—one that keeps calling you on the phone

- Potchka Organization—an organization that tries a little of this, a little of that, but doesn't really focus is an organization that is potchka-ing around. This is what I sometimes do on the weekend out in the garage.

- Saykhel Organization—an organization that uses a lot of common sense in how it executes its work and serves its customers is exhibiting saykhel

- Shtik Organization—what an organization does to differentiate itself from the pack—its shtik—also called branding

- Ver Clempt Organization—when an organization can't differentiate itself, even when it knows it is different from all other organizations, it becomes ver clempt or all choked up and sputtering as it tries to describe itself

- Zhlub Organization—an insensitive organization that cares nothing about how its employees will emotionally react to its actions is a zhlub of an organization

And for now that is the whole Megillah (which is a long complicated story).

> *Adam, exasperated, asks Eve, "What do you mean the boys don't look like me?"*–Red Buttons

MAY YOU FIND WHAT YOU ARE LOOKING FOR

TUESDAY, JANUARY 29, 2008

OFF THE CUFF

"May you find what you are looking for" is described as the third in a series of three increasingly severe Chinese proverbs that are considered curses. (The actual origins are somewhat murky). Finding what you are looking for is a curse. How is that possible? Does finding what you are looking for create a situation where you no longer need to strive, no longer need to have any initiative—is that the curse? If you find what you are looking for, is the meaning of your life gone, the notion is that humans need to have constant goals, need to feel that they can always do more, can always improve and if not, they become "empty." Is that why you read about so many unhappy rich and famous people; they have found it and have nowhere to go? While this may be the case in the ultimate sense, in our more ordinary day-to-day lives I don't buy it. You may find parts of what you are looking for, but you are, of course, never done.

NOVA, a series that appears on PBS, recently ran a segment titled, "Family that walks on all fours." It was about the hand walkers, a couple in Turkey whose five children could only walk likes quadrupeds, moving along with the assistance of both their hands and feet. Any attempt at walking on just their feet had them falling over in short order. Through MRI brain scans and genetic research, it was determined that the children suffered from a recessive mutation of a gene that caused the cerebellum, the portion of the brain that controls balance and locomotion, to be vastly undersized. The father of the impoverished family living in rural Turkey passionately states that he would give everything he has, including literally the clothes he was wearing, so his children could walk in a normal fashion. May you find what you are looking for.

Given the remoteness of the family, the children never had any medical treatment or physical therapy for their condition. One of the researchers contacted a physical therapist who brought a simple walker for the children to use and installed parallel bars that they could exercise upon and practice their balance. After a year of therapy, the children, mostly in an independent fashion, were bipedal, walking, albeit a bit shakily, on two feet. In an interview, one of the daughters, who looked to be in her late 20s, said that she wanted to meet people and find a husband so she could have a family and children of her own. I don't think her life would become empty if that happened. May you find what you are looking for.

For as long as I can remember, in New York, there has been almost a constant shortage of skilled nurses. Hospitals and other care facilities have long searched high and low for nurses to work in the metro area. Several institutions have recruited from abroad and have had particular luck recruiting in the Philippines by offering signing bonuses and even in some cases, providing housing. There is a striking article in *The New York Times* that describes Philippine nurses who are awaiting trial on charges of endangering the welfare of five chronically ill children and one terminally ill man. It is claimed that they endangered the patients in their care by walking off their jobs without sufficient notice. This was done, they stated, because of broken promises and shabby working conditions. (If the conditions were shabby for the nurses, I can't help but wonder what they were like for the patients). The patients suffered no harm however. Each of the 10 Filipino nurses could face a year in jail and the loss of their nursing licenses—their means of sustaining themselves.

Let's make the assumption (a fairly safe bet) that people who enter the nursing professions do so because of good intentions, a desire to help others and to care for those of us who are in need, and not because it is a path to quick riches. For these nurses to walk off the job without notice and potentially endanger patients, the conditions are likely to have been severe. And while it is hard to know based on the information in the paper, the prosecutor may be barking up the wrong tree and should be looking at the conditions where the nurses were from. It seems like the nurses are simply looking for a place where they can ply their trade in a professional manner and care for their patients. May they find what they are looking for.

An old fable has a mid-wife attending the birth of two children within a few hours of each other. One child born was the king's son, the other, the son of the local village baker. The mid-wife (due to reasons that I don't think you really want to know about) switched the two children at birth just to see what would happen. The king's replacement son, with the heritage of a baker, grew up with all the benefits that you would expect a king's son to have and grew into a noble ruler. The baker's replacement son, with the heritage of nobility, grew up to be one of the best bakers that the village had known under the tutelage of his loving father. May they both find what they are looking for.

Finding what you are looking for, finding contentment, in my estimation, is not a curse and never finding what you are looking for, not even a part, is no blessing.